STORE-CUPBOARD COOKERY

CLARE CONNERY

BBC BOOKS

For Clare, for her love
and understanding.

Published by BBC Books,
a division of BBC Enterprises Limited,
Woodlands, 80 Wood Lane, London W12 0TT

First published 1991
Reprinted 1991 (twice)

Illustrations © Kate Simunek 1991

Set in Itek Goudy by Ace Filmsetting Ltd, Frome, Somerset
Printed in England by Clays Ltd, St Ives plc
Cover printed in England by Clays Ltd, St Ives plc

CONTENTS

ACKNOWLEDGEMENTS

My sincere thanks to Erica Griffiths, who invited me to write *Store-cupboard Cookery* to accompany her 1991 series of *Bazaar*. I am most grateful for her help, encouragement and friendship. Without her faith and enthusiasm the book would not have been possible.

My thanks also to my wonderfully enthusiastic and understanding editor, Susan Martineau, without whose meticulous eye and patient and constructive editing my book could not have been published; to Doreen McBrien for bringing typed order out of chaos from my longhand manuscript; and, of course, to Suzanne Webber whose enthusiasm for me and my work gave me the confidence to accept the offer.

INTRODUCTION

This book is dedicated to all busy people who enjoy eating, and sometimes cooking, but because of family or business commitments, or indeed a combination of both, just don't have the time for endless hours of shopping or lengthy sessions in the kitchen.

It's a book to encourage and reassure those who quite wrongly assume that good cooking needs hours spent poring over cookery books, followed by more hours spent slaving over a hot stove. It's true that elaborate cooking may necessitate a lot of preparation and careful presentation of the ingredients; however, once you have accepted the fact that a good – even excellent – meal can be prepared in a very short space of time, if the correct kinds of combinations of food are chosen, then you will be able to create your own first-class food, freed from all inhibitions and preconceptions.

It's a book too, that, hopefully, through the speed and simplicity of the recipes, will inspire even those who don't like to cook but do so out of necessity.

It's a book for everyone who needs to produce food quickly from the store-cupboard, fridge or freezer with the added bonus that all the recipes – well, nearly all – are healthy and not outrageously expensive!

The recipes in the book are neither simply straight from the tin or packet nor openly pretentious. Many are recipes which I've enjoyed over the years, but never thought of as 'convenient' or 'perfect from the store'. Some I've acquired from my more imaginative and creative friends who have, unlike me, always had an eye for the quick and convenient, but they are all recipes which take into account the current medical advice on healthy eating and use lots of fibre and little sugar and fat. They are recipes for all the family to make and enjoy at any time of the day, whether in a hurry or not. There's everything from quick snacks and warming soups to appetising desserts and an extensive selection of main-course dishes for both the meat and non-meat eater and for all occasions.

This is a book for everyday family meals and friendly entertaining. I hope it will be food-splattered and dog-eared from constant use, that it will help your busy lifestyle become less chaotic, and indeed enable you to enjoy cooking and eating without thinking of it as a chore.

TODAY'S
STORE-CUPBOARD

I earn my living from food. I write about it, talk about it, teach people about it. Every day in life I work with it, handle and create with it, experiment and cook with it. When I'm catering I feed others with it and when I've time I also manage to eat and thoroughly enjoy it. Food is the great passion in my life and there's hardly an hour in the day when I'm not thinking about it. Indeed, when I'm particularly busy I've even been known to dream about it!

However, throughout my career I've always been faced with one major problem, a problem not unique to me, but felt by all busy people. How to run a successful career and, at the same time, feed my family quickly and easily with the minimum amount of effort. It made no difference that I was a professional food writer, experienced broadcaster and seasoned traveller, nor that I owned my own delicatessen, restaurant and catering company. The problem still remained.

Here I was with all my skill and expertise awash with food recipes and ideas, but at the end of the day I was just like everyone else, with the same problems that most people who work have – and indeed those whose job is looking after the home and family and coping with all the demands that brings – no time, and even less energy. I had tried the Indian takeaway, a variety of Chinese and pizza houses, a plethora of fish and chip shops, and none of them was really quite right.

What I needed was someone waiting at home for me, a housekeeper or an old-fashioned mum who would have tasty meals on the table at the end of a busy day – but chance would be a fine thing, and there was only me as the mum and a family to feed. There had to be another way.

There was, and it came about most unexpectedly when the BBC's *Bazaar* programme suggested I present a mini-series on cooking from the store-cupboard and write a book to go with it. Considering the project, I remembered my grandmother's kitchen, piled high with pickles, home-made preserves, smoked bacon, pickled beef, bottled vegetables and a well stocked larder. She could cook quite easily from the store-cupboard, backed up by all the fresh vegetables grown in her own garden – but, of course, she had the time. Then I remembered the days spent cooking for the deepfreeze, my big chest store-cupboard, filled with half a bullock, a sheep and a mountain of home-baked goodies, packages of pre-cooked meals, all waiting to be defrosted and whisked to the cordon bleu table. I no longer had the time or space for that carry-on and anyway, I didn't want half a cow in my kitchen albeit under ice.

My eating habits and my lifestyle, along with half the population's, had changed dramatically over the last 10–15 years. Simple, fresh, unadulterated food was once again the order of the day, but I still didn't have the time and resources my granny had. I also recalled my college days and special assignments on cooking from the store-cupboard, resulting in rather uninspired dishes with a 'samey' taste that couldn't be disguised.

Now was the time to rethink, to reconsider the store-cupboard in the light of the tremendous advances in preparation methods, packaging, techniques and design technology. To find items that would be nutritionally sound whether they came dried in a packet or liquid in a tin, jar or tetra pack; to select foods that weren't laced with harmful preservatives, additives and 'E' numbers; to find foods that were just as good preserved as fresh, but yet to combine these with a selection of carefully chosen items that could be shopped for about once a week and stored fresh in the fridge; to utilise the deepfreeze in a more efficient way – not taking up half a garage and filled with a miscellany of mystery packages, but neat, tidy, possibly combined with the fridge and housing what would help create instant meals without lengthy defrosting.

Here was today's store-cupboard. Not just a single unit but a universal triangle of dry store, freezer and fridge. What could be easier or more obvious?

I realised that cooking from the modern store-cupboard could be the answer to my own dilemma of how to produce quick nutritious meals with the minimum of fuss, preparation and cooking and shopping only once a week. The solution had been found, the challenge was waiting. What was needed was an extensive collection of well tried and tested recipes that would have a permanent place in the kitchen, that could be used every day, or in unforeseen circumstances, be quick to prepare, tasty to eat and nutritious into the bargain.

I accepted the challenge and these pages are the result. Throughout the planning, writing and recipe-testing, I made many wonderful discoveries. I found I could take shortcuts with many of my favourite dishes without spoiling them. I surprised myself by creating stunning meals from practically nothing, and I also accepted the fact that I could actually eat well from the store. It was all so exciting and just what I should have done years ago.

To produce such a book – for me, anyway – needed a major rethink and a careful study of all products currently available in the supermarkets and grocery stores. Once I had identified what I felt was nutritionally sound and valuable, I embarked on the trials and tests. As with any change of thinking and re-organisation, there often seems to be so much work involved that the easier solution would be to stay in the original place and stumble around as before, but once I had the stock identified, the recipes chosen and my basic require- ment list made, I could just about see the light at the end of the tunnel. You too, on reading the basic requirements for all three stores, might feel a bit daunted, but remember that your initial stocking up is a 'one off': once it's done and your cupboards re-arranged, all you will have to do is a simple 'top- ping up' of the dry store and freezer, along with a fresh fruit and veg. shop once a week.

This way you will be able to choose exactly what you fancy without having to think or shop at the last moment. The most you'll have to do is to select and follow a recipe. Think of the freedom: you can now work and play all day if you like and still feed yourself and your family well. It's an exciting prospect. I've already put it into action and – guess what? – the joy has returned to my kitchen.

THE HEALTHY STORE-CUPBOARD

If your first reaction to cooking from the store-cupboard is that it will be dull and boring, quickly followed by the assumption that it will also probably be unhealthy, because you think it will consist of an extensive use of packaged, tinned and refined foods high in preservatives, artificial flavourings, colours and 'E' numbers and low in nutrients, read on. It has been my main priority to see that the recipes are designed in such a way that the items required from the store-cupboard are wisely chosen and take into account current medical and nutritional advice. This suggests that for our health's sake we should eat foods low in saturated fat, sugar and salt, avoid overly refined foods and eat plenty of those high in fibre such as cereals, grains, fresh fruit and vegetables. It is also important to eat foods rich in vitamins and minerals.

The healthy store-cupboard should comprise a fine balance of all of these things, both negative and positive, and in order to include them within the book I have considered each in detail. This not only helped me to select the ingredients for the recipes with good health in mind, but should give you an understanding of those foods which are beneficial and those which are best avoided when you come to devise or choose recipes for yourself. Finally, I have also suggested some herbs, spices or seasonings you may like to invest in for your store-cupboard to ensure your meals will never be dull.

FAT

To start with there is generally too much fat in our diet. It is not always easy to identify because much of it is hidden in products like biscuits, pastry, chocolate, cakes, crisps and the like. Some fats are also thought to be more harmful than others. Saturated fat, for example, which is mostly of animal origin and found in meat and dairy products, is believed to contribute to heart disease by raising the level of blood cholesterol, which is one of the risk factors associated with this disease. But saturated fat is not only of animal origin; it is also present in some plants such as coconut and palm. Certain hard vegetable margarines can be high in saturates and are thought to be just as harmful to the body as saturated fats of animal origin. It is therefore important to read the label: when buying margarine as opposed to butter, choose the soft types made only from fats which are 'high in polyunsaturates'. The polyunsaturated variety of fats, unlike the saturated, are thought to be valuable in the diet because they actually help to reduce the blood cholesterol level. As well as some of the soft margarines, oily fish (such as mackerel and sardines) and offal are also high in polyunsaturates. Butter I keep for special dishes and occasions because, although high in saturated fat, it undoubtedly tastes better and is much more useful in cookery than any of its rivals.

There are two other groups of fats: unsaturated fats, which are present in fish and food of plant origin such as vegetables, fruit, seeds and nuts (with the exception of hazel nuts, which are high in saturates); and monounsaturated fats, which are thought to be fairly neutral in their effect on blood cholesterol. However, it has recently been suggested that the best known of the monounsaturates, olive oil, may in fact have some effect in reducing the level of cholesterol in the blood; but this theory is still being researched.

Although it is more expensive, I try to use olive oil in much of my cooking because of its wonderful flavour. I buy the cold-pressed 'extra virgin' olive oil, but keep it mainly for salad dressings because of its relatively high price. More often than not, though, for the sake of economy, I alternate between sunflower, safflower, soya and ground nut (peanut) oil, which are all high in polyunsaturates. Corn oil is too, but because of its fairly strong taste I don't use it so often. I also don't use any oil more than once for cooking as heating alters the flavour and may also change its polyunsaturates to saturates. I avoid palm and coconut oil which are both highly saturated.

MILK, CREAM AND YOGHURT

In the effort to choose store-cupboard food low in saturated fats, I use fully skimmed long-life milk or UHT (Ultra High Temperature) milk. This milk contains less than 0.3 per cent fat and has been heated for one second to 123°C to extend its life. Unopened it will keep for 1–2 months but always check the date stamp on the carton. Once opened it keeps as fresh milk. Longlife milk is always a useful store-cupboard standby, but if you prefer to use fresh milk choose semi-skimmed or skimmed. Semi-skimmed milk contains between 1.5–1.8 per cent fat which is half the fat content of full-fat, silver top milk which contains about 3.8 per cent. (Gold top has between 4.7–5 per cent fat.) Skimmed fresh milk contains less than 0.3 per cent. I also include some tins of condensed milk in my store-cupboard – my very special treat as it is not only high in fat but saturated with sugar. This I use for one of my favourite desserts, Banoffi pie (p. 121). I must also admit that I keep a baby tin of condensed milk for 'supping' when I feel the need for something sweet. I might add that I don't eat chocolates, sweets, cakes, biscuits or the like, so I feel I can permit myself this little indulgence now and again!

Real dairy cream is another treat reserved for special occasions. The long-life variety is invaluable and I keep it in my refrigerated store for the odd occasion when I feel no other substitute will do. Check the sell-by date for its shelf-life.

Whenever possible I will use yoghurt, fromage blanc or quark, a German low-fat cream cheese, instead of cream. The labelling on many yoghurts claims they are low-fat, but it is important to look at the small print and check that the fat content, which should be marked on the carton, is actually low – preferably 0.5–2 per cent. Yoghurt made from whole milk, like Greek sheep's or cow's milk yoghurt, is thicker than the low-fat varieties which are inclined to be very thin in texture. However, although it contains more fat than yoghurt made from skimmed milk, it still has less than single cream. It's best to avoid the varieties of yoghurt heavily laced with sugar, synthetic flavourings and azo dyes. If you want a yoghurt with real fruit in it, read the label and avoid those that say, for example, 'strawberry flavoured'. There are several brands that are free from additives, are low in fat and contain real fruit, and they are all now fairly widely available. It is, of course, cheaper to buy a large tub of plain yoghurt and then mix in some fresh fruit as required.

Yoghurt will have a refrigerated shelf-life of about 1–2 weeks and is certainly an important part of the modern store-cupboard. When using it as a substitute for cream and indeed cooking with it, it is important to remember that it should be whisked with hot liquid 1 tablespoon at a time and should not be allowed to boil otherwise it will curdle and not only have an unattractive appearance, but a gritty and unpleasant texture too. To prevent this and to stabilise it, put ½ teaspoon cornflour into a small saucepan and stir in 10 fl oz (300 ml) natural yoghurt. Bring to the boil, then simmer for 10 minutes, stirring all the time. This can then be used straight away, or allowed to cool and kept covered in the refrigerator for up to a week.

CHEESE

One of the most useful store-cupboard ingredients which is not only tasty but also has an infinite variety of uses is cheese. Unfortunately it is another product that is high in saturated fat. However, chosen carefully and used discreetly, it certainly is not to be completely forgotten. Most hard cheeses are high in salt as well as saturated fat, but if you choose the strongly flavoured mature Cheddar cheese, you will need to add only a small quantity to a dish for that extra flavour; and as little as ½ oz (15 g) grated Parmesan sprinkled on pasta, as you will see from the recipes, makes a small amount of fat go a long way and gives a great taste.

There are now also a number of low-fat hard cheeses on the market, such as low-fat Cheddar, which are fine for eating but not as good for cooking as they tend to have a crunchy texture, a slightly sour taste and don't melt or brown well but just remain as a deep yellow mass when heated.

Some of the softer cheeses, such as Brie, Camembert, Mozzarella, Edam and Gouda, are lower in saturated fat and the last three also melt well and are there-fore good for toppings. Other low-fat soft cheeses which are useful in the healthy larder are cottage cheese which, although without an inspired flavour of its own, combines well with fresh fruit and vegetables for an impromptu salad and mixes successfully with stronger flavourings to fill baked potatoes or to make a cheesecake.

There are a number of low-fat cream cheeses now also available which have a soft spreading texture and make good substitutes for their full-fat counter-parts in recipes like pâté, mousse and cheesecakes. They are also particularly useful in the creation of pasta and other sauces because they help to thicken them and can be boiled without separating.

Another cheese with a similar texture to that of the low-fat cream cheeses and also very low in fat is the German quark. It has a slightly sour flavour and leaves a dry after-taste on the palate, but like the cream cheeses is excellent for enriching sauces because it won't separate when boiled. It is also useful for making cheesecakes and sweet puddings and is now fairly widely available in tubs.

Fromage frais, although it translates as 'fresh cheese', is more like cream or yoghurt. It has a rich thick texture and, although slightly sharp in taste, is dis-tinctly less sour than yoghurt, which makes it the perfect accompaniment to puddings and desserts instead of dairy cream. However, it is not very good in hot liquids and can be variable in fat content, so use it cold and check the label for a brand that has a fat content under 3 per cent.

All cheeses should be stored in the refrigerator between 32–41°F (0–5°C). They should be wrapped tightly in greaseproof paper or aluminium foil. I store all of my cheeses together in a rigid container so they are all conveniently in one place. The keeping time will obviously vary depending on the type of cheese and its age, condition, and ripeness when bought. Generally, however, cheese will keep for about a week in the refrigerator without deteriorating in quality. Hard cheese will keep for several weeks but I feel it is better to avoid storing it for too long. On the whole, I prefer not to freeze cheese as it seems to lose texture and can become rubbery or crumbly when defrosted. However, hard, Cheddar-type cheese, grated and stored in sealed polythene bags, is a useful and convenient addition to the deepfreeze. It can be used while still frozen in cooked dishes or will defrost in about 30 minutes for use in sandwiches and salads.

EGGS

Another high-fat food which I've included in the store-cupboard to use sparingly, is the versatile egg. It is invaluable for all types of instant cookery and often described as the 'perfect packaged food' because it can be so quickly turned into breakfast dishes, starters, snacks, main meals, puddings and desserts, not to mention of course the innumerable variety of buns and bakes. The fat is all contained in the yolk, so obviously the white is less risky, although it is recommended that no more than three whole eggs per week are eaten in order to keep the fat intake from this source at a 'safe' level.

MEAT

Meat, although an important source of protein, vitamins and minerals, all nutrients essential to health, is also a source of saturated fat. So where I've used it in the recipes I've kept to the leaner cuts of beef, lamb and pork, trimmed of any excess fat, and used lean minced beef. In the two recipes which include sausages, I've suggested using a low-fat variety from a reputable supplier, a frankfurter which is not only low in fat but also low in additives, or a vegetarian sausage or frankfurter which is virtually fat-free and exceedingly tasty. In most cases I've removed the skin from chicken to reduce fat content. Unfortunately, the one drawback of using the lean varieties and cuts of meat is that they are generally more expensive. However, because there is also less loss in 'trimmings', they are frequently better value for money, more enjoyable to eat and a little can be made to go a long way. For instance, a stir-fried chicken or beef dish which also includes a high proportion of vegetables can make one chicken breast or fillet steak feed four people, as can a tasty chicken risotto. Lean minced beef, when combined or served with other ingredients such as rice, pasta, pulses and root vegetables, can be 'stretched' so that it not only goes further but also produces more varied, healthy and filling dishes.

In my dry store there is also a tin of corned beef, which makes very good instant curried patties when mixed with breadcrumbs or potato and seasoning and which, although itself fairly high in saturated fat, can be extended this way without increasing the fat content. I haven't included tins or jars of minced or stewed beef because the type of meat, fat content and degree of additives and preservatives isn't always clear. However, some of these could be used in a number of recipes if you were satisfied as to the quality of their content. I've avoided pies, salamis and luncheon meats too as their fat content is also high.

Meat will keep in the refrigerator at 32–41°F (0–5°C) for several days, depending on its condition when purchased, or much longer in the deepfreeze at 0°F (−18°C). When storing meat in the refrigerator it should be kept in a rigid container in its wrappings but with the wrappings opened to allow a circulation of air. This will help to extend its life. Meat should be stored at the bottom of the refrigerator to prevent any drips falling on other food. For freezing, meat should either be wrapped in aluminium foil, or put in a polythene bag, or a combination of both, and sealed well. The following table is a guide to storing and defrosting particular types of meat. It is important to thaw all meat before cooking to ensure it is cooked properly and maintains its quality. This is particularly important with poultry.

MEAT	STORAGE LIFE	DEFROSTING
BACON – vacuum-packed home-packed	6 months 5 weeks	Thaw in opened wrappings in refrigerator for 24 hours
BEEF – in joints, steaks, or chops	12 months	Thaw in opened wrappings in refrigerator for 5 hours per 1 lb (450 g)
LAMB – in joints, steaks or chops	9 months	Thaw in opened wrappings in refrigerator for 5 hours per 1 lb (450 g)
PORK – in joints, steaks or chops	6 months	Thaw in opened wrappings in refrigerator for 5 hours per 1 lb (450 g)
POULTRY – Whole bird or in pieces	12 months	Thaw in opened wrappings in refrigerator for 5–6 hours per 1 lb (450 g)
Any cubed, or minced meat, offal, and sausages	2 months	Thaw in opened wrappings in refrigerator for 4 hours per 1 lb (450 g)

SUGAR

Sugar is often described as an empty calorie because it has no nutritional value whatsoever. It is all calories, nothing else. And it doesn't matter under what guise it appears – brown sugar, white sugar, glucose, maltose, lactose, sucrose, fructose or dextrose, molasses, treacle, honey or syrup – or that the taste may vary. It serves no other purpose than to provide enjoyment, tooth decay and obesity, and frequently is eaten instead of other more nutritious foods. And yet it appears in almost all processed foods, both sweet and savoury, and in many of our home-produced dishes as well. It's in bread, cakes, pastries, biscuits, desserts and cereals, pies, pickles, sauces, ketchup, beans, jams, chutneys and marmalade. It is a cheap ingredient, an excellent preservative and helps make many foods taste more pleasant and palatable, and therefore we and the food manufacturers love it. So much so that on average we in Britain eat about 2 lb (1 kg) per head every week – quite a staggering amount, but when you consider that there are about seven spoonfuls in a glass of cola, it's not difficult to see how it can very quickly mount up. Many health pundits advise reducing our intake by half and certainly it would seem sensible to reduce it as much as possible, which is what I have done in many of the recipes used in the book. I've also selected the store-cupboard items with care, choosing as far as possible those foods which are sugar-free or are sold in their natural juice. Many fruits and vegetables have naturally occurring sugar in an unrefined form which not only gives sweetness but also provides fibre, vitamins and minerals and so is much more beneficial.

It is also a fallacy that you need sugar from a packet for energy. On the contrary, processed sugary foods make you feel tired and tend to make you want even more sugar snacks. Better sources of energy are unrefined, carbohydrate foods such as wholemeal bread, pasta, rice, potatoes and other root vegetables. So when you feel the need of instant energy or a fix of sweetness – munch some fresh fruit or raw vegetables.

SALT

Salt is constantly involved in the health food debate and, despite opinions varying greatly on the subject, it is generally believed that although a little is necessary, the average British intake of ½ oz (15 g) a day is too much. All the sodium we need for a healthy diet is naturally present in food. But salt doesn't just occur naturally; it is also added to many highly refined and processed foods, supposedly to enhance the flavour – those such as commercially pre-pared cakes, bread, biscuits and puddings, pies, bacon and pressed meats, along with tinned soups, bottled sauces and seasonings, the foods also likely to be high in fat and sugar and low in vitamins and minerals, and just the sort likely to appear in a store-cupboard!

I have therefore been very selective about what I've used in the recipes and when a tin, bottle, packet or jar is required I have used products low in or free from salt or only a small quantity of those which contain large amounts of salt such as soy sauce. When I have used such products containing salt, I've omitted salt from the recipe.

Since salt is not always directly mentioned on the labels of pre-packaged food, it is necessary to look for it under other guises. It may appear as sodium, sodium phosphate, sodium bicarbonate, sea salt, rock salt, soda, monosodium glutamate, brine or the chemical symbol Na. If the ingredients you use in a recipe seem to be salt-free, at least if you do add a little salt you will be able to tell how much. In some recipes you will see that I have suggested adding a small amount; in others where I felt it unnecessary I've left it out. At the end of the day, however, the decision is an individual one, but medical experts do cer-tainly advise reducing salt intake as they believe it is linked with high blood pressure, one of the risk factors in cardiovascular disease.

ADDITIVES

The variety of food now available to most of us has increased enormously over the last ten years. You've only got to walk around any supermarket or delicates-sen to see the extensive range of products from all over the world. Many are fresh and untampered with, but many too, particularly those that are processed and packaged, have substances added to them to extend their shelf-life, improve their appearance and flavour, and, as many manufacturers would say, to keep them safe for our consumption.

The food additives used today include preservatives, stabilisers, emulsifiers, colourants, anti-oxidants, flavour enhancers and artificial sweeteners. Not all the additives are undesirable: many are natural products and there is as yet no documented evidence that, when properly used, they will cause harm to the majority of us. However, some of the common additives are now known to create health problems ranging from allergies to stomach upsets and asthmatic attacks. It is also thought that some may even be carcinogenic.

In the UK and other EC countries, additives are given the code 'E', followed by a number.

E100s are generally colours and include the synthetic derivatives of coal tar and azo dyes. These are thought to be associated with hyperactivity, skin rashes and asthmatic attacks. They are widely used in soft drinks, ice cream, custard powder, sweets, jams and baked products.

E200–82 are mainly preservatives and acids. E250 (sodium nitrite) and E251 (sodium nitrate) are used in bacon, sausages, pies, frozen pizza and pressed meats. Although valuable in preventing botulism in tinned meats, nitrites are thought to be possibly carcinogenic.

E300–41, mainly anti-oxidants and acid regulators, are suspected of causing hyperactivity in children and a raising of blood cholesterol levels.

E400 includes emulsifiers, stabilisers, thickeners, and bulking agents.

E621 or monosodium glutamate (MSG), often referred to as the flavour enhancer, is a salty seasoning found in many convenience foods, particularly soy sauce and other oriental sauces and seasonings.

Further details, including the known effects of these additives, are available in a number of books, such as *'E' for Additives* by Maurice Hanssen, and will help you identify those best avoided.

It is important to read the label on all food products in order to find alternatives to those heavily saturated with undesirable additives, as well as to identify those which are not harmful. This will enable you to support manufacturers who are making an effort to offer products free of suspect substances. After all, as yet there is still very little scientific evidence on the long-term effect on our health of prolonged exposure to these additives, so it is prudent to be cautious.

Stocking a store-cupboard, therefore, isn't as straightforward as it might first appear. Even though there may be plenty of choice, it's a bit like walking through a maze or a minefield: not only is it easy to get lost, but making the wrong choices could have undesirable consequences. However, in the last few pages I've been more or less dwelling on the negative aspects of planning a healthy store-cupboard and providing a few signposts to guide your choice. It's fortunate, however, that the benefits of following a healthy eating pattern far outweigh the initial disadvantages and disappointments of having to forsake some of your favourite unhealthy food, and certainly in the long term enhances and even speeds up the creative catering activity in the kitchen by introducing many tasty alternatives into everyday meals.

FIBRE

One of the plus points to come out of the various medical reports such as those by NACNE (National Advisory Committee on Nutrition Education) and COMA (Committee on Medical Aspects of Food Policy in Britain) is the emphasis placed on increasing the amount of fibre in the diet. Fibre is best defined as the natural skeleton of plants – the spine that holds the leaves together, the skin and membrane in fruit and the hard cell walls which make seeds and grains feel firm to the touch. By eating plant food such as fruit, vegetables, cereals, grains, pulses, nuts, pasta and bread, you will be eating fibre and probably at the same time, though perhaps subconsciously, you will also be eating fewer animal products. This will subsequently reduce your intake of fat, and at the same time open up a whole new world not only for the cook but also for the devotee of a highly refined or high-protein diet. After all, who could resist the unusual shapes, varied texture and rich variety of the full range of technicoloured products that the plant world has to offer?

Foods made up of fibre are interesting to eat and add variety to cooking as well as being essential to health. Fibre is a vital factor in the prevention of diseases of the gut, like constipation, cancer of the colon, diverticulitis, appendicitis and diabetes, which plague Western society. It is now thought that fibre may play a significant role in the prevention of cardiovascular disease.

The importance of fibre lies in the fact that it cannot be broken down completely by the digestive system but passes directly through it, which is why it was once called 'roughage' and was believed to have no great value. However, its importance is now more fully understood. In passing directly through the digestive system it increases the weight, bulk and softness of the stools and stimulates the natural movement of the bowel to get rid of them. It also encourages the speedy passage of food through the body and has the additional advantage of helping your stomach fill up more quickly, a great benefit if you are inclined to over-indulge. If you've ever struggled through a rice-based Indian or Chinese meal and felt full half-way through, you'll understand exactly what I mean. The added bonus, therefore, is fibre as a slimming aid.

Some plant foods, rich in fibre, are thought to be more beneficial than others. Cereal fibre is one of these, and there is certainly no disputing the value of wholegrain rice, pasta and bread. However, it should be remembered that, although the benefits derived from other types of plant material are not yet fully known, it is important to eat a wide range of foods rich in fibre from both plant and cereal sources, if for no other reason than as an insurance policy!

The healthy larder thus contains an abundance of foods high in fibre. The dry store-cupboard groans with the weight and variety of rice, nuts, pasta and beans. Indeed, these are the predominant items in my store-cupboard – not the tinned soups, meats, fruit, vegetables and evaporated milk of former years.

RICE

Rice has always played an important accompanying role in my menu, basically because I'm lazy and can't be bothered with washing and peeling potatoes, particularly when I am in a hurry. Up until about ten years ago there would have been only two types of rice in my cupboard, white long-grain patna for savoury dishes and the white round short-grain pudding variety. Nowadays, however, I have extended this to include a number of other varieties.

Basmati I use for special dishes instead of patna rice because it has a slightly better flavour, though it is a little more expensive.

Short-grain rice This is the best type of rice to use for risotto. For a treat I use the special Italian round-grain Arborio rice but ordinary pudding rice works perfectly well instead. It is very absorbent and therefore perfect for this type of dish where the rice is simmered and constantly stirred in an open pan with fresh stock or water added from time to time during the cooking.

Brown (wholegrain) rice, which has not been polished or processed, retains its bran and germ and therefore its minerals and vitamins as well as its starch. It has a 'nutty' taste and a more interesting flavour than white rice. It takes a little longer to cook than the white variety, 20–40 minutes depending on the brand as opposed to 11 minutes for long-grain patna or basmati rice. However, it can always be cooking while the main dish is being prepared.

Easy- or quick-cook rice, which has been partially cooked, I never use because it is so much more expensive than the other varieties and has substantially less flavour. If you are inclined to use this type of rice because you are afraid of ending up with a sticky, stodgy mess, follow the foolproof instructions for cooking long-grain rice on p. 92 and you will not only save money but enjoy a far superior flavour too. Rice is also good cold in salads (see p. 93).

PASTA

Pasta in recent years really has been a revelation in my kitchen because it stores so well, cooks so quickly and can be made into so many exciting dishes. I just can't imagine being without it, particularly when I'm in a hurry. In the 1960s and early 1970s pasta was regarded as a 'starchy' food, along with bread and potatoes, and certainly not recommended for anyone trying to lose weight. Far from being fattening, however, this 'starchy' food is perfectly healthy as long as it's not the sweet kind. It is, after all, an 'unrefined carbohydrate' that gives a steady release of energy and is therefore particularly valuable in a healthy diet.

Wholemeal pasta is also high in fibre. Of course, it is not so healthy if you add fatty, processed and salty sauces to it, but this is not necessary as I hope you will see from the recipes on pp. 85–6. Here I give a number of recipes for quick sauces that are anything but unhealthy. There are simple sauces made from vegetables and fish as well as a few more traditional cream and meat sauces, adapted to fit into a healthy eating regime as well as being easy to make from your store-cupboard. The quantities can be halved so that the recipes can be used as a first course if desired. There are also a few suggestions for baked pasta dishes which are very useful for family meals and entertaining.

There are hundreds of different dried or fresh pasta shapes and several colours to choose from. The dried variety is the most useful in the store-cupboard and has a shelf-life of many months but the fresh, if packaged correctly, can be stored in the freezer for about 4–6 weeks. Fresh pasta tends to be more expensive, can vary in quality and, if it has been exposed too long in an open shop counter, may have dried out and lost its fresh flavour. It also has a short shelf-life unless vacuum-packaged or frozen, so shop carefully.

Wholemeal pasta is available in a limited range of shapes. It has a more chewy texture than the 'white' kind and takes a few minutes longer to cook. I find it less pleasant to eat and certainly more difficult to combine tastily with sauces as it needs a strong companion to complement its own naturally robust quality. Well-flavoured meat, fish and tomato-based sauces are fine, but the more delicate cheese and vegetable sauces are frequently lost.

I've given details of how to cook pasta on p. 85. Pasta also re-heats well in the microwave. Cover the dish it is in with non-PVC film, making sure it does not touch the food. Pierce the film a few times and heat till very hot.

PULSES

Pulses are the dried seeds of podded vegetables such as peas, beans and lentils. They are no longer only to be found in health food stores but are appearing in supermarkets and delicatessens in their own extensive and colourful variety. Nowadays there's more than red kidney beans on the shelves; you can also find butter beans, haricot beans, white kidney beans, borlotti beans, brown beans, black-eyed beans, pinto beans and chick peas, to mention just a few.

Pulse vegetables are the perfect, healthy store-cupboard food. They are high in protein and fibre, rich in minerals such as iron, potassium and calcium, and full of vitamins, particularly those of the B group. They are low in fat, filling and cheap into the bargain. They are valuable if you are trying to reduce the amount of meat in your diet, for health or for economy because they help to 'stretch' dishes, making a little go a long way. Pulses are also tasty and colourful in salads and excellent making pâtés, dips, soups and casseroles. I have included suggestions for all of these in the recipe section.

The only drawback many pulses might seem to have is the time they need to soak and cook, and the fact that you have to remember to soak them well in advance of using them and boil them fiercely for the first 10 minutes of cooking to kill the toxins. Lentils, however, either split or whole, need no soaking and will usually cook fairly quickly. Split red lentils will cook in about 20 minutes and can easily disintegrate into a purée, whereas the whole green or brown lentils will take about double the time but have a much better flavour and texture. Split peas, yellow or green in colour, the dried version of the peas we normally eat fresh, also don't require soaking and will cook in about 40 minutes; whole peas will need about 1 hour. Mung beans and black-eyed beans don't need soaking either and will cook in about 30 minutes.

Pressure cooking can considerably reduce the cooking time and completely eliminate the soaking time. When pressure cooking it is also unnecessary to boil the beans hard for 10 minutes as is done in conventional cooking in order to destroy the toxins. This is because the water temperature in the pressure cooker is so high throughout the cooking time. Lentils and split peas and beans are unsuitable for pressure cooking because they turn to a purée so quickly and can block the pressure cooker vent and safety valve.

Although these dried pulse vegetables are an excellent store-cupboard food with a shelf-life of 6–9 months, not all of them are obviously for the quick store-cupboard cook because of the pre-soaking, long cooking and necessity to plan ahead. However, there is an alternative – tinned pulses. These have already been cooked so can be used straight from the tin for either hot or cold dishes. They have two slight disadvantages. They are more expensive than the dried variety and they normally have salt and sugar added. For this reason I have suggested, where tinned pulses are used in the recipes, that they are first drained and rinsed. However, I feel that the convenience of using tinned pulses far outweighs their disadvantages. And indeed, some manufacturers are already producing low-sugar and low-salt varieties.

VITAMINS AND MINERALS

In being conscious of including as wide a variety of fibre as possible both in the diet and the store-cupboard I have ended up with a wonderfully colourful and versatile selection of rice, pasta and grains, but that doesn't complete the health story. There are other foods which provide not only fibre but many essential vitamins and minerals.

BREAD

Wholemeal bread is not only an important source of fibre but also vitamins and minerals. It should really be on the table at every meal, and contrary to the general opinion it is not fattening. Bread also freezes well and, storage space permitting, it's sensible to keep a loaf or two in stock. It is also a useful base for many different snacks which I've included in the recipe section on pp. 100–2.

FLOUR

Wholemeal and plain white flour are also important items in the store-cupboard for the thickening of some stews and for making pancakes and vegetable burgers as well as producing quick sponges and toppings when required. Wholemeal flour is more valuable nutritionally than white flour and is excellent for many recipes, but I do find it rather heavy and unpalatable in pastry and cakes and uninspiring in sauces. So in such cases I use white flour and make sure I get plenty of fibre in other ways.

NUTS

Nuts are a good source of vitamins, minerals, fibre and protein. And although they are high in calories, because they are so filling it is hard to eat too many of them either on their own as a 'nibble' or incorporated into cooked dishes. If you have ever eaten nut burgers, rissoles or roasts, you will know what I mean. Such items are not only healthy but are excellent for storage in the freezer because they take up very little space and defrost quickly. They are also fast to make. There are a number of ideas in the recipe section on pp. 97–8.

Salted peanuts, though delicious, really do have too much added salt and should be eaten sparingly.

FRESH FRUIT AND VEGETABLES

Fruit and vegetables also tell another wonderfully coloured and healthy story and, being valuable sources of fibre, minerals and vitamins, are absolutely essential in the diet, even when meals are being prepared from the store.

I'm not advocating that you store an extensive range of exotic and expensive fruit and vegetables, but a valued selection that you will enjoy and that will also be compatible with your purse. Root vegetables such as carrots, beetroot, turnips, parsnips and celeriac all store well either in a cold place or, when cleaned or pre-packed, in the bottom of the fridge. Potatoes and onions can also survive for a week or more in a cold place, while cauliflower, broccoli, celery, tomatoes, cucumber and the like really do need to be stored under refrigeration to keep their quality and nutritive value. With even a small selection of these in stock, you can prepare a variety of dishes at the drop of a hat.

Some fruits are more durable than others. Oranges, lemons and apples, for example, are good keepers, but with wise and careful shopping and storage, pears, bananas, nectarines and plums will all last the week too.

Frozen fruit and vegetables are also good store-cupboard buys. They are packaged under such strictly hygienic conditions and frozen so fast after picking that they will surprisingly often contain more minerals and vitamins than their fresh equivalents. Moreover, unlike their tinned counterparts, they have no sugar, salt or colourings added and retain their texture.

Salad Leaves One of the most important vegetable items for me, particularly when I am in a hurry, is a selection of salad leaves. They add colour, flavour, texture and nutrients to any meal and require little or no preparation. Some are cheaper and easier to come by than others, like the cabbage head-type lettuces such as 'Iceberg' and 'Webb's Wonderful' and the round floppy varieties. Cos lettuce, such as 'Little Gem', with its long crisp-textured and well-flavoured leaves, not only tastes good but also keeps extremely well. I find the more tightly packed the leaves, the better the value and shelf-life.

There are several cabbages which are also useful as salad leaves, notably Chinese leaves, an elongated, pale green, frilly cabbage with very tender leaves, and pak-choi, a small, oriental cabbage with bright green leaves and thick white stalks. Both of these can be finely shredded and used for salads or stir-fry dishes. The more familiar Dutch white and red cabbages, although delicious for coleslaw-type salads, are inclined to be rather strong, even bitter in flavour and are better cooked rather than used solely as salad leaves.

Some of the other leaves which I use from time to time are not only more difficult to find but are inclined to be more expensive. However, you may like to try them. These are the very attractive-looking lettuces like the frilly pink and maroon lollo rosso, the browny oakleaf and the strikingly handsome frisée with its sprawling head of shaggy green leaves. Radicchio, a small tightly packed chicory from Italy, goes a long way, lasts well and in small pieces brings life and colour to any salad. Many supermarkets and greengrocers are now selling packets of these leaves in different combinations.

Most salad leaves need careful handling and storage in the refrigerator to ensure that they will last as long as possible. I remove the dead or wilted outside leaves and then put the rest of the head either inside a polythene bag or in a rigid salad container and store in the bottom of the fridge. The firm-headed cabbage-type leaves can also be stored this way. I wash the leaves only as I require them otherwise they will wilt, go soggy and become inedible. The softer loose-leaved lettuces will keep refrigerated for about 4 days, while 'Iceberg' lettuce, Chinese leaves and other cabbage varieties will certainly last for about 7 days and ensure that, even if you shop just once a week, you will have enough until the next shopping spree.

HERBS, SPICES AND SEASONINGS

In addition to a wide range of nutritionally valuable foods in my dry and refrigerated stores, there is a selection of items that are present solely because they enhance whatever food is available and add sparkle and colour to even the dullest tinned product. I am referring to herbs, spices and seasonings. Once sold only in specialist shops, they are now available in extensive variety in most supermarkets and grocery stores. Keeping a stock of dried herbs and spices will ensure that you have some to hand throughout the year, but in the recipes I have suggested the use of fresh herbs as well, not only for their lively flavours but also for their colour and texture. I grow some of those I use most frequently like parsley, mint, chives, tarragon, marjoram, thyme and oregano in pots on my windowsill or just outside my back door, and when their season is nearly over I harvest them and store them in small packages in the freezer for use throughout the winter. Many greengrocers and garden centres are now selling potted herbs as well as packets of seeds and they are very easy to grow and tend and don't need either a garden or much space. I have given a list on pp. 29–30 of the herbs, spices and other seasonings that I find most useful in my store-cupboard, many of which are required for various recipes in this book.

THE WORKING STORE-CUPBOARD

ORGANISING THE STORE-CUPBOARD

With this wide variety of fresh, dried and tinned produce available in the modern healthy store-cupboard, there is no excuse for either not being able to produce a meal at the last minute or producing one which is dull and boring, particularly if you use the recipes which follow. No specialist equipment, with the exception of a liquidiser or food processor, is required and in addition to a dry, well-organised and well-ventilated cupboard to store all the dried, tinned and packeted goods, only a refrigerator and small freezer (or frozen-food compartment in the refrigerator) are required.

THE DRY STORE-CUPBOARD

The dry store-cupboard should be organised in such a way that you know exactly where to put your hand on what you need without having to rummage every time. Keep the soups, sauces, pickles and seasonings together, the tinned fruit, vegetables and meats in separate rows and the nuts, grains and cereals in a separate place. The space will dictate how this arrangement will best work. But keep the shelves clean and tidy and make a note each time an item is used so that it can be replenished on the next shopping trip.

THE REFRIGERATOR

The refrigerator likewise should be kept clean and well ordered with salad leaves and soil-free vegetables stored at the bottom in polythene bags, rigid polythene containers or the salad drawer or crisper provided. I also store perishable fruit like plums, pears and nectarines in the fridge, space permitting, or in a cold well-ventilated cupboard. Dairy and cooked dishes should be stored at the top of the fridge, always with raw meats below them in sealed containers where possible to prevent cross-contamination between raw and cooked food. Keep all foods covered, for example in polythene bags or in lidded plastic containers. Try to avoid using aluminium foil as all too often, because you can't see through it, you're left with many mystery packages that would have been of value if discovered in time!

The fridge should be thoroughly washed and tidied at least once a week and any drips or spillages cleaned immediately. In order to obtain the longest possible life from your perishable food, always buy the best-quality produce and store in the fridge at a temperature of 32–41°F (0–5°C). It is important to be aware of the temperature inside your fridge, and if it is not already equipped with a thermometer it's advisable to buy one and fit it yourself: they aren't expensive.

THE FREEZER

The freezer too should be kept clean, well organised and free from frost so that it will work efficiently. Its temperature should be 0°F (−18°C). The amount of fresh food and pre-cooked items that you will be able to store in the freezer will obviously depend on its size and your requirements. I find it particularly useful for things like bread, frozen vegetables, fresh pasta, chicken breasts and joints, lamb chops, minced beef, cod fillets, ice cream and peeled prawns. I also keep a few pastry cases for quiche, vol-au-vents ready for filling and a selection of home-made sauces like tomato. There are also usually some grated cheese, breadcrumbs, croûtons, soups, stocks and fresh herbs. As you can see from the list, although I no longer have a chest freezer I do have a reasonable-sized upright one, mainly because my work often provides food I can't always use immediately.

STOCKING UP

The secret in having any form of store-cupboard is to make it work for you rather than the other way round. One way to do this is to make a list of the ingredients you are most likely to use in your cooking and shop for those only rather than leaving the choice to be dictated by the supermarket shelves or the empty feeling you might just happen to have in your stomach. I always find it fatal to shop when I'm hungry as I always buy lots of things I don't actually need or want.

It is very difficult to give suggestions for stocking someone else's store-cupboard because each person is an individual and therefore has different requirements as well as likes and dislikes. However, there are a number of items that are necessities in any store-cupboard. Some will be used frequently, others much less so, but each plays an important role in helping you to create meals without having to shop for them each time.

I have based the following lists on all the recipes in the book. Obviously some things, particularly in the fridge, such as fruit and vegetables, will have seasonal variations. I've left those to you and just included the basics. The 'alcoholic additions' are really for a special treat so do not feel you must have all the suggested bottles in the store. However, an inexpensive way of stocking them all would be to buy miniatures. The lists are only a guide, but I hope they will be of some help.

When you read the lists you may find them a little daunting because I've included absolutely everything. A less expensive way to build up your store-cupboard is to choose a selection of recipes that you feel would be useful and buy what you need to make them. This way you can try the recipes and choose exactly which items you are going to stock up on. You will almost certainly have some in stock already. One of the great benefits of the store-cupboard is that you don't have to buy everything at once, you can keep adding bits and pieces and build it up over a period of months, experimenting as you go.

Some of the ingredients are listed by exact measures and sizes, for example in the use of tinned foods. This is because the exact size of tin was used in the recipes. If you cannot find the exact size just use the nearest available. It would be so helpful for cooks if all tins had standard sizes! Other items I have specified more generally in 'packets' because less than a whole packet is required in the recipe.

THE DRY STORE-CUPBOARD

TINNED PRODUCE:

1 × 7½ oz (213 g) plum tomatoes
3 × 14 oz (397 g) plum tomatoes
1 × 15 fl oz (425 ml) tomato juice
2 × 7 oz (198 g) sweetcorn kernels
1 × 7½ oz (213 g) red kidney beans
1 × 15¼ oz (432 g) red kidney beans
1 × 7½ oz (213 g) haricot beans
1 × 14 oz (400 g) chick peas
1 × 15.2 oz (430 g) butter beans
1 × 10.4 oz (295 g) condensed
   consommé
1 × 10.4 oz (295 g) condensed
   cream of celery soup
1 × 10.4 oz (295 g) condensed
   cream of chicken soup
1 × 10.4 oz (295 g) condensed
   cream of mushroom soup
1 × 10.4 oz (295 g) vegetable soup
1 × 10.4 oz (295 g) tomato soup
1 × 14.5 oz (415 g) pear halves

1 × 11 oz (312 g) mandarin oranges
1 × 11 oz (312 g) raspberries
1 × 12 oz (340 g) pineapple pieces
1 × 11 oz (312 g) gooseberries in
   syrup
1 × 13.5 oz (383 g) pineapple rings
1 × 11 oz (312 g) peach halves
1 × 11 oz (312 g) sliced mango in
   syrup
1 × 15 oz (425 g) ready-made custard
1 × 14 oz (397 g) condensed milk
2 × 4½ oz (120 g) sardines in oil
2 × 11 oz (312 g) smoked mackerel
2 × 7 oz (200 g) tuna fish in oil
1 × 7 oz (200 g) salmon in oil
1 × 4 oz (105 g) smoked mussels in
   oil
1 × 2½ oz (65 g) anchovies in oil
2 × 7 oz (198 g) corned beef
1 × 7 oz (198 g) ham

DRY GOODS

Apple juice
Orange juice
Long-life skimmed milk
Packet croûtons, plain or garlic
Packet short-cut macaroni
Muscovado or demerara sugar
Caster sugar
Small packet cornflour
Bicarbonate of soda
Cream of tartar
Bag plain flour

Bag wholemeal flour
1 packet (8) trifle sponges
Packet meringue nests
Packet meringue shells
Small jar whole baby beetroot
Sunflower oil
Bottle ginger in syrup
1 packet jasmine tea
Bulgur wheat
Porridge oats
Long-grain patna rice

Short-grain pudding rice
Shortbread biscuits
Cigarette russe biscuits
1 × 4¾ oz (135 g) packet lemon jelly
1 × 8 oz (225 g) block dark chocolate
Chocolate milk flake
1 tub or packet gelatine powder
1 packet nibbed almonds
Selection of nuts (unsalted peanuts, walnuts, Brazils, pecans, hazels or cashews)
Packet small unsalted peanuts
Packet dry-roasted peanuts
Mixed dried fruit (apricots, peaches, pears, dates, figs, prunes, bananas)
Packet sultanas
Glacé cherries
1 × 4½ oz (126 g) packet instant mashed potato mix

1 × 2½ oz (65 g) packet instant mashed potato mix
1 bag plain potato crisps
Selection of pasta (spaghetti, noodles, plain or spinach tagliatelle and lasagne
1 × 8 inch (20 cm) pre-cooked pastry shell
Small packet desiccated coconut
Packet or jar approximately 8 frankfurters
Packet (12) Breton or Breton-style pancakes
Jar crunchy peanut butter
Black olives
Green olives
Pickled dill cucumbers
Whole green lentils
Split red lentils

SAUCES AND SEASONINGS

Clear honey
Mushroom ketchup
Worcestershire sauce
Mango chutney
Tomato ketchup/sauce
Tomato purée
Salad cream
Mayonnaise
Dijon mustard
English mustard powder
Curry paste
Tahini paste
Soy sauce
Tabasco sauce
1 × 9 oz (250 g) bottle Indian tikka marinade or sauce

Bottle lemon juice
Apple cider vinegar
Red wine vinegar
Distilled malt vinegar
Salt
Vegetable stock cubes (low-salt)
Beef stock cubes (low-salt)
Chicken stock cubes (low-salt)
Dried herbs
  Basil
  Bay leaves
  Chives
  Marjoram
  Mint
  Oregano
  Parsley

Tarragon
Whole spices
  Caraway seeds
  Whole cloves
  Blades mace
  Nutmeg
  Black peppercorns
  Sesame seeds
Ground spices
  Chilli powder
  Cinnamon
  Cloves
  Coriander
  Cumin

Curry powder
Ginger
Mace
Nutmeg
Paprika
Turmeric
Alcoholic additions
  Beer
  Port
  Rum
  Dry sherry
  Medium sherry
  Dry white wine

THE REFRIGERATOR

Block vegetable margarine
Sunflower margarine
Butter
Long-life cream
Greek-style natural yoghurt
Low-fat plain yoghurt
Fromage frais
Quark
2 × 4½ fl oz (135 ml) apricot fools
Stilton cheese

Cheddar cheese
Edam cheese
Gruyère cheese
Feta cheese
Piece or small carton grated
  Parmesan cheese
4–8 oz (100–225 g) low-fat cream
  cheese
Eggs, size 3
Lean back bacon

VEGETABLES

Bean sprouts
Carrots
Cauliflower
Celery
Courgettes
Cucumber

Garlic
Root ginger
Leeks
Mushrooms
Onions
Spring onions

Parsnips
Green pepper
Red pepper
Potatoes
Tomatoes

SALAD LEAVES	FRUIT	FRESH HERBS
Cress	Apples	Basil
Lettuce and other	Bananas	Chives
salad leaves	Grapefruit	Marjoram
	Grapes	Mint
	Nectarines	Oregano
	Oranges	Parsley
		Tarragon

THE FREEZER

Selection of bread (white, brown, wholemeal, pitta, French stick – quartered)
Breadcrumbs (white and brown)
Selection of chopped fresh herbs
1 × 8 inch (20 cm) cooked savoury pastry shell

1 × 1½ lb (750 g) packet frozen peas
1 × 4 oz (113 g) packet frozen peas
Vanilla ice cream
1 lb (450 g) blackberries
1 × 13 oz (368 g) packet frozen puff pastry

FISH	CHICKEN	MEAT
Cod steaks	Chicken breasts	Lamb cutlets
Smoked mackerel fillets	Chicken drumsticks	Pork chops
Shelled prawns		Lean sausages
		Slice rump steak
		Lean minced beef

In designing the recipes for this book and suggesting the items necessary not only to create them but also other dishes of your own design, I have planned that after the initial stocking-up you should only need to shop once a week. This will enable the dry store-cupboard to be topped up and the perishable items stored in the refrigerator and freezer to be replenished. Obviously if you are only buying a few items at a time, then it will take longer to establish your store, but once it is to your liking then you too can join the once-a-week, topping-up brigade. Happy and healthy cooking.

NOTES ON THE RECIPES

Follow either imperial or metric measures for the recipes, not a mixture of both.

All spoon measures given are for either imperial or metric measuring spoons. Such spoons are readily available and give accurate measurements for small quantities.

Plain flour has been used in the recipes unless otherwise stated.

All recipes serve 4 except where otherwise stated.

Three different sizes of onions have been used in the recipes. Their approximate weights are as follows:

Large	7–8 oz (200–225 g)	
Medium	5 oz (150 g)	
Small	3 oz (75 g)	

I have added salt to some of the recipes that I think benefit from it and have left it out of others. If you are not in the habit of using this seasoning, its omission will in no way detract from the flavour of the dish.

Where sizes of cartons, packets or tins have been given they have been taken directly off the products used in testing the recipes. Use the nearest size available to you.

THE RECIPES

SOUPS AND STARTERS

Soups and starters enable the store-cupboard cook to be wonderfully creative because both can be made out of so very little. Tins of soup can be quickly opened and dressed – or should I say disguised? – with a dash of sherry, white wine, cream or even brandy, or camouflaged by the addition of a few sautéed mushrooms, some cubes of crispy bacon, crunchy croûtons of bread and a heavy dusting of chopped parsley or snipped chives.

For the more discerning store-cupboard cook there's always the creative blending of complementary tins to conjure up some very individual tastes and textures, or indeed the mixing of tinned fruit and vegetables to produce the closest likeness possible to the real thing. But convenient as tinned and packet soups are, there's no getting away from the fact that they all, with a few exceptions, have a very distinctive and 'samey' taste which is hard to mistake or disguise. They are good for the occasional 'cheat' but no substitute for the real thing whose creation calls upon the talents of the inventive cook.

A few miscellaneous vegetables lurking in the fridge along with some herbs and spices, perhaps a little rice, or even some pasta or beans, can quickly be turned into an appetising concoction to cheer the most jaded palate. A dish like this can be used as anything from a simple first course to a main meal, needing nothing more than a good loaf of bread, some farmhouse cheese and a piece of perfect fruit as companions.

Such soups are also very quickly prepared and can generally be cooked in 30–40 minutes. They don't always need an elaborate stock, but a home-made one prepared from left-over vegetables, a poultry carcass or bones will certainly make all the difference in the world. When or if you have the time, try to make a large amount of stock and pack it away in your freezer in 5 fl oz (150 ml), 10 fl oz (300 ml) and 1 pint (600 ml) quantities, ready to use for soup, sauces and stews as the need arises. There's very little effort involved in the actual preparation and it's a good way to use up left-overs.

Stock cubes, if chosen carefully so that they are low in salt and artificial additives, are also a good standby, but not always necessary as some of the vegetable-based soups provide enough flavour on their own.

Starters too can be created out of very little, with nothing more than a dash of imagination. A few seasonal vegetables cut into thick sticks and served with an instant pâté of chick peas; tuna fish or mushrooms make as healthy and sophisticated a first course as you might want, while a simple half grapefruit grilled with a little sugar, port and ginger can be instantly transformed from a breakfast basic into an entertaining special.

The first course is my favourite part of the meal and the one I always find time both to create and enjoy. Indeed, on many occasions I've often combined several starters and turned them into my main course.

THE CHEAT'S COLLECTION

An interesting collection of soups can be quickly made by combining one or even two good-quality tins of soup with a few additional ingredients. The first recipe could be made with condensed cream of mushroom soup if preferred.

EACH SERVES 4

CELERY AND STILTON SOUP

1 × 10.4 oz (295 g) tin condensed cream of celery soup
10 fl oz (300 ml) skimmed milk
1 tablespoon dry sherry (optional)
2 oz (50 g) Stilton cheese, crumbled
2 tablespoons snipped chives

Combine the soup, milk and sherry in a saucepan, stirring to blend. Heat through, then add the Stilton, stirring until it is just beginning to melt. Sprinkle with the chives and serve hot but not boiling.

QUICK MINESTRONE

1 × 10.4 oz (295 g) tin vegetable soup
1 × 10.4 oz (295 g) tin tomato soup
10 fl oz (300 ml) vegetable stock
1 oz (25 g) short-cut macaroni
Salt and freshly ground black pepper
1 oz (25 g) Parmesan cheese, grated

Combine the tins of soup in a large saucepan, add the stock and macaroni and simmer for 15 minutes or until the pasta is cooked. Season with salt and freshly ground black pepper and serve sprinkled with grated Parmesan cheese.

CREAM OF MUSHROOM SOUP

1 × 10.4 oz (295 g) tin condensed cream of mushroom soup
10 fl oz (300 ml) skimmed milk
2 oz (50 g) button mushrooms, finely sliced and fried in 1 tablespoon sunflower oil

Combine the soup and milk in a saucepan, stirring well to blend. Add the prepared mushrooms, bring to the boil and serve.

BEANFEAST SOUP

A big healthy soup made with whatever varieties of tinned beans are available in the store-cupboard. A great standby for emergencies. Serve with pitta or wholemeal bread.

SERVES 4

2 tablespoons sunflower oil
1 large onion, finely chopped
2 cloves garlic, crushed
1 tablespoon ground turmeric
½ teaspoon ground cinnamon
1 teaspoon dried mint
1 × 7½ oz (213 g) tin red kidney beans
1 × 7½ oz (213 g) tin haricot beans
7½ oz (213 g) tinned chick peas
3 oz (75 g) whole green lentils
2 pints (1.2 litres) vegetable stock
Freshly ground black pepper
5 fl oz (150 ml) Greek-style natural yoghurt
A little salt (optional)
2 tablespoons finely chopped parsley

Heat the oil in a large saucepan and gently fry the onion and garlic until soft but not coloured. Add the turmeric, cinnamon and mint and continue to fry for a few minutes to draw out their flavour.

Drain the tins of beans and peas, rinse the pulses under cold running water and drain again. Add to the saucepan. Stir in the lentils along with the vegetable stock and pepper. Bring to the boil, cover, then simmer for 30 minutes.

Remove about 5 fl oz (150 ml) of pulses along with a little stock from the pot and liquidise until a thick purée is formed. Allow to cool slightly, then add the yoghurt and process to blend. Gradually stir this creamy mixture into the hot but not boiling soup. Adjust the seasoning, adding a little salt if necessary. Heat through gently and serve sprinkled with finely chopped parsley.

Rag-bag Soup

A rich hearty soup which uses up all your left-over raw vegetables. Make it with a combination of whatever you have, either finely diced or thinly shredded, balancing the flavours so that no one vegetable predominates. You can add red lentils to enrich the liquid, but pasta or rice are equally tasty. Alternatively some tinned beans such as red kidney or white haricot can also be used.

SERVES 4

2 tablespoons sunflower oil
2 carrots, diced, approx. 8 oz (225 g)
1 medium onion, chopped, approx. 5 oz (150 g)
2 leeks, thinly sliced, approx. 4 oz (100 g)
2 sticks celery, thinly sliced
1 large potato, diced, approx. 8 oz (225 g)
2 oz (50 g) red lentils or rice or pasta or tinned kidney or haricot beans, drained and rinsed
2 pints (1.2 litres) vegetable stock
Freshly ground black pepper
1 tablespoon finely chopped parsley

Heat the oil in a large saucepan and add the prepared vegetables. Press a piece of greaseproof paper or foil on top of them and cook very gently, stirring occasionally, for 15–20 minutes or until the vegetables are beginning to soften. This is a process called 'sweating' which draws out the juices from the vegetables and heightens the flavour.

Add the lentils, rice, pasta or tinned beans of your choice along with the vegetable stock and pepper. Bring to the boil, then reduce the heat, cover and simmer for a further 20 minutes or until the vegetables are very tender. Check the seasoning and adjust as necessary.

Spoon the soup into bowls and serve garnished with the chopped parsley.

MINTED GREEN PEA SOUP

A delicious, light, summery soup with a bright green colour and distinctive flavour.

SERVES 4

1 tablespoon sunflower oil
1 medium onion, chopped
Pinch dried mint or 2–3 sprigs fresh mint
1¼ pints (750 ml) vegetable or chicken stock
1½ lb (750 g) frozen peas
Juice ½ lemon
Salt to taste
Freshly ground black pepper
4.4 fl oz (125 ml) carton fresh or long-life single cream or milk
Fresh mint leaves to garnish (optional)

Heat the oil in a large saucepan and gently fry the onion until soft but not coloured. This will take about 3 minutes. If using fresh mint, set aside 1 sprig to use as a garnish. Now add the stock, peas, dried or fresh mint, lemon juice, salt and freshly ground pepper to the pan. Bring to the boil, then reduce the heat, cover and simmer for 15–20 minutes or until the peas are very tender.

Blend until smooth in a liquidiser or food processor, or pass through a sieve or vegetable mouli. Return the purée to the saucepan, bring to the boil again, reduce the heat and add three-quarters of the cream or all of the milk (if using) and stir to blend. Warm through without boiling.

Serve in a soup tureen or individual soup bowls. Pour the remaining cream (if using) on top of the soup and swirl to give a marbled effect. Garnish with a sprig of fresh mint, if available.

FRENCH ONION SOUP

A thick and substantial soup which is really a meal in itself. If French bread is not available, use thick pieces of ordinary white bread cut to a similar size. Gruyère is the best type of cheese for cooking because it doesn't go stringy, but Cheddar is less expensive.

SERVES 4

FOR THE SOUP
1 lb (450 g) onions
2 tablespoons sunflower oil
1 × 10.4 oz (295 g) tin condensed consommé
1½ pints (900 ml) water
Salt and freshly ground black pepper

FOR THE GARNISH
4 slices French bread
2 oz (50 g) Gruyère or Cheddar cheese, grated

Thinly slice the onions. Heat the oil in a large saucepan and fry the onions until a rich golden brown colour, but take care not to burn them.

Pour the tinned consommé on top of the onions, add the 1½ pints (900 ml) water and stir to blend well. Season with salt and pepper. Bring to the boil, then reduce the heat until the soup is just simmering. Cover and cook for 30 minutes.

Cut the French bread into diagonal slices 1 inch (2.5 cm) thick. Toast lightly on both sides. Place in the bottom of individual ovenproof bowls. Pour on the boiling soup and scatter the grated cheese thickly on top. Finish under a hot grill until the cheese is melted, brown and bubbling. Alternatively cook in a pre-heated oven at gas mark 7, 425°F (220°C), for 10–15 minutes.

TOMATO, PEAR AND TARRAGON SOUP

A fruit and vegetable mixture with a delicately balanced flavour and more than a hint of summer. Equally good hot or cold.

SERVES 4

2 tablespoons sunflower oil
1 medium onion, roughly chopped
1 × 14 oz (397 g) tin plum tomatoes
1 × 14½ oz (415 g) tin pear halves, drained
2 pints (1.2 litres) vegetable stock
1 tablespoon dried tarragon
Pinch grated nutmeg
Salt and freshly ground black pepper
1 teaspoon brown sugar
Parsley sprigs or a few fresh tarragon leaves, if available

Heat the oil in a large saucepan and fry the onion until soft but not coloured. Add the tomatoes and their juice along with the drained pear halves. Pour on the stock and season with the tarragon, nutmeg, a pinch of salt, some pepper and the sugar.

Bring to the boil, chopping through the mixture with a spoon to break up the tomatoes and pears. Cover, reduce the heat and simmer for about 20 minutes or until the mixture is pulpy and the flavours are well blended. Put the mixture into a liquidiser or food processor and blend until smooth.

Return to the saucepan and bring to the boil again, adjusting the seasoning as necessary. Serve garnished with sprigs of parsley or a few fresh tarragon leaves.

CURRIED PARSNIP SOUP

A delicately flavoured and inexpensive soup with just a dash of curry to give it a taste of the East.

SERVES 4

2 tablespoons sunflower oil
1 medium onion, chopped
2 cloves garlic, crushed
1 medium parsnip, diced
1 level teaspoon curry powder or paste
2 pints (1.2 litres) vegetable or chicken stock
Freshly ground black pepper
2½ fl oz (65 ml) cream or milk or natural yoghurt
2 tablespoons finely chopped parsley

Heat the oil in a large pan and fry the onion and garlic over a gentle heat for a few minutes until soft but not coloured. Add the diced parsnip and stir to combine with the onion and garlic. Lay a piece of greaseproof paper or foil on top of the vegetables and continue to cook over a gentle heat for about 10 minutes.

Remove the cover, then stir in the curry powder or paste, blending well. Fry for 1 minute to allow the curry flavour to develop. Stir in the stock, season with pepper, bring to the boil, then reduce the heat and simmer until the parsnip is tender. This will take about 20 minutes.

Blend until smooth in a liquidiser or food processor, or pass through a vegetable mouli.

Return the soup to the pan, bring to the boil again and add the cream, milk or yoghurt. Sprinkle with the chopped parsley and serve.

GAZPACHO ANDALUZ

This famous cold Spanish soup, often referred to as 'liquid salad', is brightly coloured and full of flavour and goodness. Tinned tomatoes not only speed up the preparation time but also often provide better colour and flavour than fresh ones.

SERVES 4

1 small onion, finely diced
1 small red pepper, de-seeded and finely diced
1 small green pepper, de-seeded and finely diced
2 inch (5 cm) piece cucumber, finely diced
1 clove garlic, crushed
1 × 14 oz (397 g) tin plum tomatoes
1 × 15 fl oz (425 ml) tin tomato juice, chilled
1 tablespoon clear honey
2 tablespoons apple cider vinegar or red wine vinegar
Finely ground black pepper
1 tablespoon finely snipped chives
1 packet small plain or garlic-flavoured croûtons, to serve

Prepare the onion, peppers and cucumber and put about 2 tablespoons of each into a large soup tureen or serving bowl. A glass bowl is ideal because it shows the colours up wonderfully well.

Put the remaining diced vegetables into a liquidiser or food processor along with the garlic and tomatoes and blend until a smooth purée is formed. Add the chilled tomato juice, honey, vinegar and black pepper and process again until well mixed.

Pour the liquidised soup on top of the diced vegetables in the soup bowl and chill until very cold. To speed up the chilling process a few ice cubes can be added to the soup.

Garnish with snipped chives and serve croûtons separately to be sprinkled on top of the soup.

HOLLAND PARK MUSHROOM PÂTÉ

This earthy-flavoured pâté is rich, tasty, filling and incredibly popular. Not only that, it's quick to make and inexpensive. Serve with fingers of hot toast or warm pitta bread.

SERVES 4

1 tablespoon sunflower oil
1 oz (25 g) salted butter
1 small onion, finely chopped
8 oz (225 g) open-cap mushrooms
1 teaspoon ground coriander
4 oz (100 g) low-fat cream cheese
1 tablespoon fine brown breadcrumbs
1 teaspoon mushroom ketchup
Dash Worcestershire sauce
Freshly ground black pepper

Put the oil and butter in a large frying-pan and heat gently until the butter has melted. Cook the onion in this until soft but not coloured.

Wipe and slice the mushrooms and add to the pan. Continue to cook gently until they are soft and most of the moisture has been driven off. Add the ground coriander and fry for a few minutes to develop the flavour. Cool slightly before turning into a liquidiser or food processor.

Add the remainder of the ingredients and process thoroughly until a fine black-flecked purée is formed. Start and stop the machine several times and push the mixture well down on to the blades so that it may become evenly blended. The pâté can be processed until very smooth or left with a little texture, depending on your taste.

Spoon into either one or four individual serving dishes, levelling the top. Cover and chill before serving.

A Trio of Fish Pâtés

Tinned tuna fish, salmon, sardines and kippers are wonderful standbys in the store-cupboard, as are a few frozen fillets of smoked mackerel. They can be quickly turned into a tasty pâté for a snack or an elegant starter. Serve in individual pots or in mounds on a bed of mixed salad leaves with hot toast or pitta bread. For special occasions the pâté can be piled into empty lemon shells or mixed with hard-boiled egg yolk and used to fill the cavity of the egg white.

EACH SERVES 4

Tuna or Salmon Pâté

2 × 7 oz (200 g) tins tuna fish or salmon, drained
2 tablespoons lemon juice
5 tablespoons natural yoghurt or fromage frais or single cream
Salt and freshly ground black pepper

Sardine or Kipper Pâté

2 × 4½ oz (120 g) tins sardines or kipper fillets in oil or tomato sauce, drained
1 tablespoon lemon juice
2 tablespoons finely chopped fresh parsley (optional)
¼ teaspoon ground mace
2 tablespoons natural yoghurt or fromage frais or single cream

Smoked Mackerel Pâté

Approximately 8 oz (225 g) mackerel fillets, skin and bones removed,
or 2 × 4 oz (110 g) tins smoked mackerel in oil, drained
4 tablespoons mayonnaise or natural yoghurt
1 tablespoon lemon juice
Freshly ground black pepper

Simply put all the ingredients in a liquidiser or food processor and blend until smooth. Adjust the seasoning and consistency as required.

HUMMUS

A traditional Middle Eastern dish made from chick peas and tahini – a sesame seed paste sold in jars by health food stores and the delicatessen section of some supermarkets. Using tinned chick peas and a food processor makes this a very quickly prepared dish for a nutritious starter or snack. Serve as described below or, alternatively, as a dip, surrounded by crudités – a selection of raw vegetables cut into sticks; or, if small, like radishes and cherry tomatoes, left whole. Many vegetables are perfect for this purpose, including carrots, celery, cucumber, peppers, fennel, courgettes, radishes and cauliflower and broccoli florets. Choose 4–6 varieties of contrasting colours, shapes and textures.

SERVES 4

1 × 14 oz (400 g) tin chick peas
1 clove garlic, crushed
3 tablespoons lemon juice
5 fl oz (150 ml) tahini paste
Freshly ground black pepper
1 teaspoon salt
5 fl oz (150 ml) olive or sunflower oil
6 tablespoons set natural yoghurt
Lemon wedges, to garnish
Paprika to garnish

Drain and rinse the chick peas and put into a liquidiser or food processor with the garlic, lemon juice, tahini paste, pepper and salt. Process until a very smooth paste is formed, gradually adding the oil. Finish by adding the yoghurt.

Spoon on to individual serving plates, making a well in the centre. Pour a little extra olive oil in the middle, garnish with a lemon wedge and a sprinkling of paprika, and eat by scooping up with pieces of warm pitta bread.

A Leafy Duet

A selection of salad leaves such as iceberg, round and cos lettuce, Chinese leaves, curly endive, oak leaf, sorrel, spinach, watercress, chicory and radicchio can form the basis of a great variety of dishes from starters and snacks to main-course meals. Packets of mixed leaves can now be bought in many large supermarkets and used to enliven the more familiar and less costly varieties.

Here are two of my favourite recipes using salad leaves, which should give you ideas for many more. All that's required are some ingredients from the store-cupboard, perhaps a few left-overs from the fridge, and, of course, a little imagination.

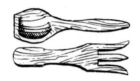

Mixed Salad Leaves with Bacon, Croûtons and Feta Cheese

EACH SERVES 4

A selection of salad leaves as available, washed and dried
4 oz (100 g) lean back bacon, diced and fried
4 oz (100 g) Feta or other cheese, cubed
1 packet plain or garlic croûtons
Freshly ground black pepper
4 tablespoons French dressing (see p. 47)

Mix the salad leaves together in a large bowl. Add the bacon, warm or cold, cheese and croûtons and season with the pepper. Sprinkle over the French dressing and toss gently. Divide between 4 plates and serve at once.

ROASTED STILTON WITH MIXED SALAD LEAVES

4 × 1½ in (4 cm)-thick diagonally-cut slices French bread
4 oz (100 g) Stilton cheese, rind removed and sliced
4 small tomatoes, sliced
A selection of salad leaves as available, washed and dried
4 tablespoons French dressing (see below)

Place the pieces of bread on a baking sheet and cover with half the Stilton. Arrange a thinly sliced tomato on each and top with the remaining cheese. Cook under a hot grill until the cheese is bubbling and crusty.

Combine the salad leaves in a bowl, pour on the dressing and toss. Divide between 4 plates and set a slice of Stilton bread on top. Serve immediately.

FRENCH DRESSING

FOR 10 FL OZ (300 ML) DRESSING

10 fl oz (300 ml) olive or sunflower oil
3½ fl oz (100 ml) wine or distilled malt vinegar
2–4 cloves garlic, peeled and crushed
Salt and freshly ground black pepper

Put all of the ingredients into a clean container with a tight-fitting lid. Seal well and shake vigorously until an emulsion is formed. Taste for seasoning. If the dressing tastes too oily, add a little extra salt which will help 'cut' the oil. The dressing will keep in the refrigerator for several weeks.

COCOTTE EGGS

This simple dish of eggs baked in cream, cooked in individual ovenproof dishes or 'cocottes', is incredibly versatile. Spicy tomato sauce (see p. 98) may be used instead of cream and finely shredded cooked bacon, ham, chicken, smoked salmon or vegetables such as cooked spinach, mushrooms or cheese placed in the cocottes under the eggs.

½ oz (15 g) sunflower margarine or butter
Additional ingredients of your choice (optional: see introduction)
4 eggs
Salt and freshly ground black pepper
1 tablespoon single cream or spicy tomato sauce per egg

Pre-heat the oven to gas mark 5, 375°F (190°C). Butter 4 individual ovenproof dishes and place any additional ingredients, if you are using them, on the base. Break an egg on top, season, and spoon over the cream.

Set the dishes on a baking sheet and bake in the oven for 8–9 minutes or until the egg whites are set but the yolks are still slightly soft.

Serve on a plain doyley on an under plate and eat with a teaspoon.

GARLIC MUSHROOMS

Mushrooms are such complete and versatile little packages that it takes only a few additional ingredients to turn them into a special treat. Here garlic is the predominant seasoning and complements the 'meaty' flavour and texture of the mushrooms to perfection. Serve with fingers of hot toast or pitta bread.

SERVES 4

2 tablespoons sunflower oil
2 oz (50 g) butter or sunflower margarine
4 large cloves garlic, crushed
10 oz (275 g) button mushrooms
Pinch salt
Freshly ground black pepper
2 tablespoons finely chopped parsley

Combine the oil and butter or margarine in a large frying-pan and heat until the butter has melted. Gently fry the garlic over a low heat until soft, taking care that it doesn't burn.

Wipe the mushrooms, leaving the stalks attached – they are full of flavour. Add the mushrooms to the pan and fry gently until they are hot and sizzling. Season to taste, sprinkle on the parsley and serve immediately.

GRILLED GRAPEFRUIT WITH GINGER AND PORT

Grapefruit halves prepared in segments, soaked in port, dotted with butter, sprinkled with demerara sugar and chopped ginger and grilled make a deliciously refreshing starter. This is particularly tasty when the 'ruby red' or 'blush' grapefruit are available. Tinned grapefruit segments can be prepared in the same way. Serve with melba toast.

SERVES 4

2 large grapefruit
4 tablespoons port or sweet sherry
4 tablespoons demerara sugar
4 teaspoons finely chopped preserved ginger
1 oz (25 g) butter or sunflower margarine

Prepare the grapefruit by cutting them in half. Then, using a grapefruit knife or a small serrated fruit-knife, cut round the edge of the grapefruit, releasing the flesh from the shell and leaving the white pith attached to the shell rather than the flesh. Now cut between each grapefruit segment, keeping the knife close to the membrane which naturally divides the fruit into sections. If this is done correctly, you should be able to remove the membrane from each grapefruit half in one piece, which makes eating much less messy. Set on a baking sheet or in an ovenproof dish.

Pour 1 tablespoon port or sherry on each grapefruit half, sprinkle with 1 tablespoon sugar and dot with ginger and butter or margarine.

Cook under a hot grill for approximately 5 minutes or until warmed through and brown on top. Alternatively bake in a pre-heated oven at gas mark 6, 400°F (200°C), for 10–15 minutes. Serve immediately in individual dishes or soup cups.

THE MAIN COURSE

The main course of any meal can be as substantial or light as your appetite and purse require. It can consist of meat and two veg., veg. and no meat, fish, rice, beans, pasta or eggs. It can be a whole meal in a pot or a collection of little meals all on one plate, because the healthy cook of today has no rigid constraints. Even when cooking from the store-cupboard there is, after the initial shopping and stocking of course, an abundance of foods with which to create, from the dry store, the fridge or the freezer.

What you choose to store will obviously depend on your individual eating habits and requirements, but with today's modern methods of preservation and packaging, heavy disguises and additions, even to tinned products, are seldom needed. Herbs, spices and seasonings, however, can enhance any food and store-cupboard food is no exception.

Most of the main-course recipes in this book concentrate on chicken, fish, vegetables, beans, pasta and pulses, with a few for lean beef and the more choice cuts of lamb and pork. The meat used can be either fresh or frozen, whichever is most convenient. If you use frozen meat make sure it is defrosted before cooking. If you are freezing meat yourself, make sure that it has been carefully wrapped to prevent it from being damaged by the extreme temperature in the freezer. See p. 14 for more on freezing and defrosting meat.

This is a healthy and varied collection of recipes, most of which can be prepared in a trice and many of which are suitable not only for family meals but for entertaining as well. In some of the recipes I have used or suggested some of the wide variety of tinned, packet and bottled sauces, spice and seasoning combinations, and special recipe sauces such as tikka and satay. The supermarkets are quite groaning under the weight and variety available and it is difficult to know which are good, bad or acceptable until they have been tried. Read the label carefully, go for a well-known brand name to start with and see which is most suited to your taste. Some are very good, even though expensive.

There are also many long-life tinned and packeted ready meals now available and these, like the cook-chill variety, are certainly worth stocking up with should you want occasionally to avoid cooking altogether. Quality can vary enormously, so it is important to choose a reputable make.

Cooking should be enjoyable and fun; if it's all hard work, the joy is lost, so balance your meals, prepare a few, buy in a few, and occasionally eat out. That way there will always be variety and pleasure around your table.

FISH

ITALIAN TUNA

A rich Italian tuna and spaghetti dish, this is quick and easy to prepare, particularly since all the ingredients are straight from the store-cupboard.

SERVES 4
---

2 tablespoons sunflower oil
1 medium onion, finely chopped
1 clove garlic, crushed
2 pinches chilli powder
8 black olives, stoned
1 × 7 oz (200 g) tin tuna fish in oil, drained
1 × 14 oz (397 g) tin plum tomatoes
5 fl oz (125 ml) chicken stock
1 teaspoon dried oregano
Freshly milled black pepper
Pinch salt
Pinch sugar
12 oz (350 g) spaghetti
A few tinned anchovy fillets (optional)
Freshly grated Parmesan cheese, to serve

Heat the oil in a frying-pan and fry the onion and garlic until soft. Add the chilli powder and continue to fry for a minute to develop the flavour. Add the olives, tuna fish, tomatoes, chicken stock, oregano, black pepper, salt and sugar, stirring well to combine. Bring to the boil, then reduce the heat and cook for about 15 minutes or until the mixture is rich and thick.

Meanwhile cook the spaghetti in a large saucepan of boiling salted water with a few drops of oil added. Cook for about 12 minutes or until the pasta is just tender. Drain well and arrange on 4 individual serving plates. Divide the tuna mixture between each, arranging it on top of the pasta. Garnish with a few pieces of anchovy if liked and serve with freshly grated Parmesan cheese.

GRATIN OF SEAFOOD

A useful store-cupboard standby which can be quickly made from frozen cod and prawns, a few mushrooms and either a home-made or commercially prepared cheese sauce. The home-made variety, although quick to prepare, will not be as convenient – neither will it be quite as expensive! If the prawns are to be omitted, use an extra 2 oz (50 g) mushrooms. The gratin can be served as either a first or main course by varying the portions accordingly. Accompany with salad and wholemeal bread.

SERVES 4

FOR THE CHEESE SAUCE
15 fl oz (450 ml) milk
Piece onion
6 peppercorns
1 blade mace
1 bay leaf
1 oz (25 g) sunflower margarine
1 oz (25 g) plain flour
Freshly ground black pepper
3 oz (75 g) Cheddar cheese, grated
1 oz (25 g) Parmesan cheese, grated (optional)

FOR THE FISH
1 lb (450 g) fresh or frozen cod, defrosted if frozen
2 oz (50 g) button mushrooms
½ oz (15 g) sunflower margarine
4 oz (100 g) prawns, shelled (optional)
Juice ½ lemon

Pre-heat the oven to gas mark 4, 350°F (180°C).

Warm the milk with the onion, peppercorns, mace and bay leaf, then remove from the heat and leave to infuse for about 5–10 minutes. This will give it an excellent flavour which will add to the taste of the finished dish.

Meanwhile prepare the fish. Cut the cod into finger strips or pieces, removing any bones. Slice the mushrooms. Lightly grease 4 individual ovenproof dishes with the margarine. Divide the fish and the mushrooms between the dishes and scatter with the prawns (if using). Pour the lemon juice on top.

Now complete the sauce. Melt the margarine in a saucepan, stir in the flour and cook gently for a few minutes. Remove from the heat. Strain the milk and gradually add to the margarine and flour mixture, stirring constantly to prevent lumps from forming. Return the saucepan to the heat, season with the pepper and add two thirds of the Cheddar cheese. When the cheese has melted, spoon over the fish. Mix together the remaining Cheddar and Parmesan (if using) and sprinkle on top. Bake in the oven for 20–25 minutes or until the fish is cooked and the sauce is bubbling and golden in colour.

TUNA AND BEAN SALAD

Tuna steak and red kidney beans moistened with mayonnaise and flavoured with spring onions, served with sliced new potatoes and tomatoes on a bed of mixed salad leaves. Tinned salmon can also be used for this recipe and a little sliced apple combines well with it.

A selection of salad leaves forms the base of this salad: the more variety, the more interesting the salad.

SERVES 4

A selection of salad leaves, washed and dried
1–2 × 7 oz (200 g) tins tuna fish steak in brine or oil, drained
1 × 7½ oz (213 g) tin red kidney beans, drained and rinsed
3 tablespoons mayonnaise or salad cream
3 spring onions, finely sliced
12 small new potatoes, scrubbed, boiled until tender and sliced
4 tomatoes, quartered
Lemon wedges to garnish

Arrange the salad leaves on 4 large plates. Mix the tuna with the kidney beans and mayonnaise or salad cream and stir in half the spring onions. Arrange the sliced potatoes in an overlapping circle in the centre of the salad leaves. Pile the tuna and bean mixture on top. Arrange the tomatoes on the leaves around the tuna to form a circle. Sprinkle the entire salad with the remaining spring onions and garnish with a lemon wedge.

CRUNCHY TUNA AND APPLE SALAD

Tinned tuna fish is one of the most versatile and high-quality store-cupboard foods. It can be served hot or cold in casseroles, kedgerees and pâtés. Here it is combined with apple, celery, potatoes and beetroot to make a substantial main-course salad. Serve with crusty bread.

SERVES 4

1 × 7 oz (200 g) tin tuna fish in oil, drained
1 dessert apple, peeled, cored and diced
2 sticks celery, diced
3 cooked potatoes, diced
1 × 4 oz (113 g) packet frozen peas, cooked
Freshly ground black pepper
Lettuce leaves to garnish, washed and dried
4 small whole beetroot, drained and diced
4 medium tomatoes, sliced

FOR THE DRESSING
4 tablespoons mayonnaise or salad cream
4 tablespoons natural yoghurt
1 small clove garlic, crushed
1 tablespoon lemon juice
Freshly ground black pepper

Combine the tuna, apple, celery, potatoes and peas in a large bowl, mixing to combine and lightly break up the tuna.

Mix the ingredients for the dressing and pour over the tuna mixture. Season with freshly ground pepper and toss gently to coat.

Arrange a circle of lettuce leaves on 4 individual plates. Divide the tuna salad between the plates, piling it in the centre. Arrange the diced beetroot around the edge of the tuna, scattering a few pieces over the top. Lay the tomatoes in overlapping slices on the lettuce.

CHEESY GRILLED COD

A deliciously quick and tasty dish made from either fresh or frozen fish steaks, covered with a savoury topping of cheese, breadcrumbs and mustard and grilled until golden.

SERVES 4

*4 fresh or frozen cod steaks, weighing approximately 14 oz (400 g),
defrosted if frozen
1 tablespoon sunflower oil
½ small onion, grated
1 oz (25 g) fresh breadcrumbs
2 oz (50 g) Cheddar cheese, grated
1 oz (25 g) sunflower margarine
1 teaspoon mustard powder
Pinch salt
Freshly ground black pepper
2 tomatoes, sliced*

Pre-heat the grill.

Lay the cod steaks on a lightly oiled baking sheet. Brush with a little oil and grill under a medium heat for about 5 minutes before turning and grilling for a further 3 minutes on the other side.

While the fish is cooking, prepare the topping. Combine the grated onion, breadcrumbs, cheese, margarine and seasonings in a bowl, mixing well to blend. Lay the sliced tomatoes on top of the fish and press the cheese mixture over their surface. Grill for a further 3 minutes until the cheese topping is golden-brown and the tomatoes cooked.

TUNA FISH LASAGNE

An interesting and tasty alternative to meat lasagne. Sheets of lasagne which require no pre-cooking not only speed up the preparation but are also less troublesome. Commercially prepared cheese sauce can also be used instead of the home-made variety – just add a little lemon juice for a sharper flavour. This recipe requires 1¼ pints (750 ml) sauce. Serve with a tossed green salad and garlic bread (see p. 95).

SERVES 4

FOR THE SAUCE
1 pint (600 ml) milk
Piece onion
1 bay leaf
1 oz (25 g) sunflower margarine
4 tablespoons plain flour
2 oz (50 g) Cheddar cheese, grated
Juice ½ lemon
Freshly ground black pepper

FOR THE FISH LASAGNE
1 tablespoon sunflower oil
1 small onion, finely chopped
6 oz (175 g) mushrooms, sliced
2 × 7 oz (200 g) tins tuna fish in oil, drained
Pinch salt
Freshly ground black pepper
3 oz (75 g) plain or spinach lasagne that does not need pre-cooking
2 large tomatoes, skinned, de-seeded and chopped
2 oz (50 g) Cheddar cheese, grated
1 oz (25 g) Parmesan cheese, grated (optional)

Pre-heat the oven to gas mark 6, 400°F (200°C).

Begin by making the sauce. Warm the milk with the onion and bay leaf, then remove from the heat and leave to infuse for about 10 minutes.

Meanwhile prepare the fish filling. Heat the oil in a large frying-pan and fry the onion until soft but not coloured. Add the mushrooms and continue to fry. Stir in the tuna fish, salt and pepper.

Now complete the sauce. Melt the margarine in a saucepan, stir in the flour and cook gently for a few minutes. Remove from the heat. Strain the infused milk and gradually add to the margarine and flour mixture, stirring constantly to prevent lumps from forming. Return the saucepan to the heat and add the cheese, lemon juice and pepper.

Lightly oil a 10 ×6 ×2 in (25 ×15 ×5 cm), 2½ pint (1.5 litre) dish and pour a little sauce over the base. Place a layer of lasagne on top, spread half the tuna mixture over the pasta, cover with lasagne and half the remaining sauce. Repeat with the remaining tuna, pasta and sauce. Scatter the chopped tomatoes on top. Combine the Cheddar cheese with the Parmesan, if using, and sprinkle on top of the tomatoes. Bake in the oven for 30–40 minutes or until bubbling hot and golden brown.

PACIFIC PIE

A truly quick, convenient, store-cupboard dish which makes excellent eating when time is short. Mushroom soup also works well instead of chicken soup. Serve the pie with boiled brown rice (see p. 93).

SERVES 4

2 × 7 oz (200 g) tins tuna fish in oil, drained
1 × 10¼ oz (295 g) tin condensed cream of chicken soup
1 × 4 oz (113 g) packet frozen peas, cooked and drained,
or 1 × 7 oz (198 g) tin sweetcorn, drained
3 tomatoes, sliced
1 × 3 oz (75 g) packet plain potato crisps, lightly crushed
3 oz (75 g) Cheddar cheese, grated

Pre-heat the oven to gas mark 4, 350°F (180°C).

Break the tuna fish into large flakes and mix with the chicken soup and peas or sweetcorn. Turn into a shallow ovenproof casserole dish and cover with the sliced tomatoes. Scatter the potato crisps and cheese on top and bake in the oven for 30 minutes or until bubbling hot.

BAKED COD IN SPICY TOMATO SAUCE

Cod steaks, either fresh or frozen, lend themselves wonderfully to being cooked in a sauce. In this recipe I have cooked the steaks in a smooth, spicy, home-made tomato sauce flavoured with orange and olives. However, for total convenience you don't even have to make your own sauce, because the fish will also taste delicious if baked in one of the following: 2 × 11 oz (300 g) jars tomato or tomato-based sauce; 2 × 8.82 oz (250 g) cartons Cheddar cheese or mushroom sauce, topped with a little extra cheese and browned under the grill to finish; 1 × 10¼ oz (295 g) tin condensed mushroom soup to which a few sliced and fried mushrooms have been added; or 1 × 14 oz (397 g) tin ratatouille for extra special flavour and texture. The possibilities are endless. All that's required is a little imagination!

New potatoes or brown rice (see p. 93) and green beans go well with this dish.

SERVES 4

---

4 thick fresh or frozen cod steaks, defrosted if frozen

FOR THE SAUCE
1 tablespoon sunflower oil
1 medium onion, finely chopped
1–2 cloves garlic, crushed
1 × 14 oz (397 g) tin plum tomatoes
2½ fl oz (65 ml) vegetable stock
1 teaspoon sugar
Pinch dried basil
Juice and grated rind ½ orange
Pinch salt
Freshly ground black pepper
8 green olives (optional)
1 tablespoon finely chopped parsley

Pre-heat the oven to gas mark 6, 400° F (200° C).

Arrange the cod steaks in a shallow ovenproof dish, then prepare the sauce. Heat the oil in a saucepan and fry the onion and garlic until soft but not coloured. Add the tomatoes, stock, sugar and basil. Bring to the boil, then reduce the heat and simmer for 15 minutes to reduce the liquid and concentrate the flavour. Purée the sauce in a liquidiser or food processor until smooth. Stir in the orange juice and rind, season with salt and pepper and pour over the fish. Add the olives to the dish if using, cover with foil and bake in the oven for 20–30 minutes or until the fish is cooked. Remove the foil, sprinkle with parsley and serve.

SALMON QUICHE

This instant store-cupboard dish is certainly one of the classics. Tinned salmon or tuna baked in a pre-cooked pastry shell with a simple custard can be made and on the table in 30 minutes, and with the availability of good-quality commercial pastry cases there's no excuse for getting a take-away meal on the pretext that everything takes too long or requires too much effort! Try it and see the result for yourself. Serve with a green salad.

SERVES 4

1 × 8 inch (20 cm) pre-cooked savoury pastry flan case
1 × 7 oz (200 g) tin salmon in oil, drained
1 pickled dill cucumber, sliced
2 eggs
5 fl oz (150 ml) carton single cream or natural yoghurt
Pinch salt
Freshly ground black pepper
2 oz (50 g) Cheddar cheese, grated

Pre-heat the oven to gas mark 5, 375°F (190°C).

Place the pastry flan case on a baking sheet. Turn the drained salmon or tuna into it and flake with a fork while spreading over the base of the flan case. Scatter the sliced pickle on top. (Sliced olives, mixed pickles or tinned anchovy fillets could be used instead of the pickled dill cucumber.)

Beat the eggs and cream or yoghurt in a bowl, season with the salt and pepper and pour over the fish. Sprinkle the cheese evenly over the surface and bake in the oven until lightly set and golden in colour. This will take 25–30 minutes. Serve hot or cold.

CHICKEN

CHICKEN SATAY

A highly spiced dish from Indonesia, not for the faint-hearted! Tender pieces of meat are soaked in a hot, peanut-based marinade, threaded on to skewers, grilled and served with an equally hot, nutty satay sauce. I have used chicken in this recipe but cubes of tender beef, pork or vegetables could also be used.

Serve with brown rice (see p. 93) and a crisp green salad, and accompany with satay sauce (see p. 61). For convenience a tinned or bottled satay sauce is certainly a help in making both the marinade and the sauce.

SERVES 4

4 chicken breast fillets, skinned and cut into 1 inch (2.5 cm) cubes

FOR THE SATAY MARINADE
1 tablespoon sunflower oil
2 teaspoons ground coriander
2 teaspoons ground cumin
1 teaspoon ground turmeric
¼ teaspoon chilli powder
1 teaspoon grated lemon rind
1 teaspoon muscovado sugar
4 oz (100 g) crunchy peanut butter
2 tablespoons desiccated coconut
Juice 1 lemon

Combine the marinade ingredients in a large bowl. It will be very stiff. Stir in the chicken pieces and leave in the refrigerator for about 1 hour if possible.

When you are ready to cook, loosely thread the chicken pieces on to 4 large or 8 small skewers, pressing pieces of the remaining marinade on to the meat. It will all look rather lumpy, but that's fine. Lay the skewers on a lightly oiled, foil-lined baking sheet and grill under a pre-heated moderate grill for 15 minutes, turning several times during the cooking. Cook until the meat is cooked through and beginning to brown.

SATAY SAUCE

Hot, spicy and nutty, this can be served as a sauce or dip for pieces of plain grilled meat or vegetables, as well with chicken satay (see p. 60).

SERVES 4

2 tablespoons sunflower oil
1 small onion, grated
2 oz (50 g) dry-roasted peanuts, ground in a nut mill or liquidiser
¼ teaspoon chilli powder
1 tablespoon soy sauce
1 tablespoon muscovado sugar
4 tablespoons desiccated coconut
Juice and grated rind ½ lemon
1 teaspoon cornflour blended with 10 fl oz (300 ml) chicken stock or water

Heat the oil in a saucepan and fry the onion gently with the ground peanuts and chilli powder for about 10 minutes. Add the rest of the ingredients, bring to the boil and cook for a further 10 minutes to develop the flavour.

CUCUMBER RAITA

A mild-flavoured and cooling Indian yoghurt dish, the perfect accompaniment to any spicy and highly seasoned meat, fish or vegetable. I prefer to use Greek-style sheep's milk yoghurt as I find it less rich and creamy.

SERVES 4

15 fl oz (450 ml) natural yoghurt
4 inch (10 cm) piece cucumber, peeled and coarsely grated
2 tablespoons finely chopped fresh mint or bottled mint sauce
Pinch ground cumin
Freshly ground black pepper
Squeeze lemon juice

Put the yoghurt in a bowl. Beat lightly with a fork or whisk until smooth. Add the remaining ingredients and mix in. Cover and refrigerate until required.

CHICKEN TIKKA KEBABS

Cubes of tender chicken marinated in an Indian sauce flavoured with lemon juice, ginger and cumin. There are many excellent varieties of commercially prepared tikka sauces and marinades now available from delicatessens and supermarkets: this dish uses one not only for speed and convenience but also for flavour. Serve on a bed of brown rice with a crisp green salad or stir-fried vegetables (see p. 107) and cucumber raita (see p. 61).

SERVES 4

FOR THE MARINADE
2 tablespoons sunflower oil
1 onion, finely chopped
2 cloves garlic, finely chopped
1 × 9 oz (250 g) bottle Indian tikka marinade or sauce
Juice 1 lemon
1 oz (25 g) unsalted peanuts
3 oz (75 g) sultanas
1 tablespoon sugar

FOR THE KEBABS
4 chicken breast fillets, skinned
1 large red or green pepper
8 large mushrooms, quartered

Heat the oil in a frying-pan and fry the onion and garlic until soft. Put into a bowl with the bottled tikka marinade or sauce, the lemon juice, peanuts, sultanas and sugar. Stir well to combine.

Cut the chicken breasts into ¾ inch (2 cm) cubes and toss in the sauce. Leave to marinate for about 20 minutes.

Cut the pepper in half, remove the seeds and pith and cut the flesh into ¾ inch (2 cm) pieces. Wipe and quarter the mushrooms. Pre-heat the grill.

Thread the marinated chicken and vegetables on to 8 skewers, alternating the pieces of meat and vegetables. Most of the marinade will stick to the meat. Cook under a hot grill for about 10 minutes, turning during the cooking. Baste with any remaining marinade. Grill until the sauce is beginning to char and the chicken is completely cooked through.

SAVOURY STUFFED PANCAKES IN CHEESE SAUCE

One valuable store-cupboard dish which is all but forgotten, with the exception of once a year on Shrove Tuesday, is pancakes or crêpes. Originally devised to use up the butter, eggs and milk before the Lenten fast, the crêpe is most versatile in that it can be served at any time of the day with whatever filling, flavouring or topping takes your fancy. And what's more, if you don't want to make them for yourself, you can now buy Breton or Breton-style pancakes ready to use in vacuum-sealed packs from most good delicatessens and supermarkets.

Serve these savoury pancakes with a crisp green salad.

SERVES 4

FOR THE SAUCE
2 oz (50 g) sunflower margarine
2 oz (50 g) plain flour
1 pint (600 ml) chicken stock
4 fl oz (120 ml) milk or cream
1 egg yolk
Squeeze lemon juice
Freshly ground black pepper
4 oz (100 g) Cheddar cheese, grated

FOR THE PANCAKES AND FILLING
2 tablespoons sunflower oil
1 onion, finely chopped
6 oz (175 g) mushrooms, finely chopped
12 oz (350 g) cooked chicken, finely diced
2 tablespoons finely chopped parsley
Pinch salt
Freshly ground black pepper
12 large thin pancakes

Pre-heat the oven to gas mark 6, 400°F (200°C).

Begin by making the sauce. Melt the margarine in a saucepan, stir in the flour and, when thoroughly blended, gradually add the chicken stock, stirring all the time to prevent the sauce from 'lumping'. Cook for a few minutes until the sauce thickens. Blend the milk or cream with the egg yolk. Remove the sauce from the heat and stir in the yolk and cream mixture. Season with the lemon juice and freshly ground black pepper. Keep warm while preparing the filling.

Heat the oil in a large frying-pan and fry the onion and mushrooms until cooked. Stir in the chicken and parsley and bind with 2–3 tablespoons of the prepared sauce. Season further if necessary.

Divide the chicken and mushroom filling between the 12 pancakes, roll up and place in a lightly buttered shallow ovenproof dish. Pour over the rest of the sauce, sprinkle with the cheese and bake in the oven for 20–30 minutes or until the pancakes are piping hot, the sauce bubbling and the cheese topping golden brown.

Chicken Koftas with a Spicy Yoghurt Sauce

Koftas are Middle Eastern meatballs for which there are numerous recipes. They can be made from beef, lamb, veal or chicken and can be large or small for main dishes, savouries or cocktails. They are plainly fried and served, as here, with a simple sauce or baked in a more elaborate concoction.

Rice and a green salad go well with the koftas, and instead of the yoghurt sauce you could serve them with cucumber raita (p. 61) or spicy tomato sauce (p. 98). The koftas can also be served in warm pitta bread pockets stuffed with chopped lettuce, tomato and onion salad, and moistened with the sauce.

A food processor or liquidiser is required for this recipe.

SERVES 4

FOR THE KOFTAS
4 chicken breast fillets, weighing approximately 1 lb (450 g) when skinned
2 oz (50 g) white bread
2 oz (50 g) unsalted peanuts, hazelnuts or pine nuts
2 teaspoons ground cumin
1 teaspoon ground cinnamon
Pinch ground cloves
½ teaspoon ground mace
2 teaspoons ground coriander
Salt and freshly ground black pepper
2 tablespoons finely chopped fresh parsley or coriander
1 egg
Flour for dusting
2 tablespoons sunflower oil
Lemon wedges to garnish

FOR THE SPICY YOGHURT SAUCE
Approximately 10 fl oz (300 ml) natural yoghurt
2 cloves garlic, crushed
Juice 1 lemon
½ teaspoon ground cumin
1 teaspoon paprika
½ teaspoon ground cinnamon
1 tablespoon finely chopped fresh parsley or coriander

Skin the chicken and cut roughly into pieces. Put the bread and nuts in a food processor or liquidiser and process to form fine crumbs. Add the chicken pieces, cumin, cinnamon, cloves, mace, ground coriander, salt, pepper and parsley or fresh coriander and process again until very finely minced. Add the egg and blend until well mixed. With wet hands form this paste into 30 balls about the size of a walnut. Roll each ball lightly in flour.

Heat the oil in a large frying-pan and fry the meatballs for about 10 minutes, turning frequently, until cooked through and an even golden-brown colour.

While the meatballs are cooking, prepare the sauce by combining all the ingredients in a bowl and whisking to blend. Pour into a serving bowl.

When the chicken koftas are cooked, drain on kitchen paper. Serve with lemon wedges, and hand round the spicy yoghurt sauce separately.

STIR-FRIED GINGER CHICKEN WITH VEGETABLES

A complete meal in 30 minutes: tender strips of chicken breast stir-fried with ginger, peppers, carrot, bean sprouts and spring onions in a rich spicy sauce. The main thing to remember with stir-fries is to make sure all of your ingredients are prepared before you begin the cooking. The cooking time is so fast! Delicious with wholegrain rice (see p. 93).

Any appropriate pre-prepared tinned or bottled sauce can be combined with the chicken and vegetables for convenience. However, it is important to check the ingredients on the label to ensure that there are no additives which could be detrimental to your health. If a reliable make is used, the result, although perhaps not quite as good as if it were home-made, will still be tasty and certainly convenient.

SERVES 4

FOR THE SAUCE
2 cloves garlic, crushed
2 tablespoons cornflour
1 tablespoon paprika
2 tablespoons dark soft brown sugar
1 teaspoon ground ginger
4 tablespoons soy sauce
½ teaspoon Tabasco sauce
2 tablespoons medium sherry (optional)
1 pint (600 ml) chicken stock or water

FOR THE STIR-FRY
2 chicken breasts, weighing approximately 1 lb (450 g) when skinned and boned
1 medium red pepper
1 medium green pepper
1 large carrot
8 spring onions
2 tablespoons sunflower oil
4 oz (100 g) bean sprouts
6 thin slices fresh root ginger, peeled

TO SERVE
8 oz (225 g) brown rice, boiled (see p. 93)

Combine all the ingredients for the sauce in a measuring jug ready to add to the pan when the chicken and vegetables are cooked. If you aren't in a rush, marinate the chicken breasts for about 30 minutes in the sauce mixture before frying: this will enhance the flavour.

Cut the skinned and boned chicken into thin finger strips. Halve the peppers lengthways and remove the seeds and pith. Cut into strips about 1½ inches (4 cm) long and ⅛ inch (3 mm) thick. Cut the carrot to a similar size and shape. Trim the spring onions and cut into 1½ inch (4 cm) lengths, reserving 4 pieces from the white end for the garnish.

Prepare the garnish by making very fine knife cuts along the length of each reserved piece of onion towards the root end, but leaving the root end intact so that the pieces are held together. Soak in a bowl of iced water until required: the strips will separate and curl like the petals of a flower.

Heat the oil in a large frying-pan. Lift the chicken strips out of the sauce if you have been marinating them and fry until cooked and just beginning to colour. This will take about 3 minutes. Add the peppers, carrot, spring onions, bean sprouts and root ginger, and continue to fry for a further few minutes, tossing and turning the contents of the pan.

Stir the sauce to make sure that it is well blended and pour into the pan. Bring to the boil and cook for a few minutes, stirring all the time to cook and thicken the sauce and combine the flavours. Serve with boiled brown rice garnished with the spring onion 'flowers'.

VARIATIONS

Try making up your own stir-fry recipe by using whatever ingredients are available in your fridge or freezer. Pork fillet or frying steak could be used instead of chicken and any combination of firm-textured vegetables. Courgettes, parsnips, green beans, baby sweetcorn, leeks and mushrooms are all very suitable, with or without meat – just increase the quantities of vegetables as necessary if you're cooking a meatless stir-fry. Nuts and seeds of all varieties can also be added to ring the changes. Peanuts, sesame and pumpkin seeds can all be used or the more expensive cashew and pine nuts for special occasions.

CHICKEN DRUMSTICKS IN BARBECUE SAUCE

Chicken drumsticks are useful finger food for barbecues and economical for family meals. They can be bought in large bags ready for the freezer at premium prices and are a useful store-cupboard standby, either fresh or defrosted. They cook quickly under the grill or in the oven and are particularly good marinated in and served with a spicy barbecue sauce. Lamb and pork chops and spare ribs of pork are also excellent cooked this way. And the sauce is perfect with sausages and burgers. This recipe gives details for a home-made barbecue sauce, but for convenience a bottled or cartoned variety can be used instead. Baked jacket potatoes and a green salad are nice with the chicken drumsticks for a main course.

SERVES 4

FOR THE BARBECUE SAUCE
1 tablespoon sunflower oil
1 small onion
2 cloves garlic, crushed
1 tablespoon dried basil
2 tablespoons tomato ketchup
1 × 14 oz (397 g) tin plum tomatoes
4 tablespoons soy sauce
10 fl oz (300 ml) chicken stock
4 tablespoons clear honey

FOR THE CHICKEN
8 chicken drumsticks
1 tablespoon sunflower oil

Grate the onion into a large bowl and add the remainder of the sauce ingredients, breaking up the tomatoes. Stir to blend. Make 2–3 diagonal slashes through the skin of each chicken drumstick, place in the sauce and leave to marinate for at least 15 minutes so that the flavours can impregnate the meat.

Pre-heat the grill to moderate. Lay the marinated drumsticks on a lightly oiled baking sheet and grill, basting with some of the sauce and turning occasionally, until the chicken is thoroughly cooked. This will take about 25–30 minutes.

While the chicken is cooking, put the remaining sauce into a saucepan and bring to the boil, then reduce the heat and cook steadily. Serve the drumsticks with the bubbling hot sauce.

QUICK CORONATION CHICKEN SALAD

Of all the recipes for cold chicken dishes, perhaps the one for Coronation chicken is the most famous, and indeed the most adulterated. Created by the Cordon Bleu School of Cookery in London in honour of the Coronation of Queen Elizabeth II, this cold poached chicken dish with its rich mayonnaise flavoured with the essence from a curried concoction is a sheer delight. Although this recipe cannot compare with the original it is still a good substitute – and quick too.

SERVES 4

FOR THE CORONATION SAUCE
10 fl oz (300 ml) best-quality bottled or home-made mayonnaise
1 tablespoon tomato purée
1 tablespoon curry paste
1 tablespoon lemon juice
1 teaspoon paprika

FOR THE CHICKEN
4 cold cooked chicken breast fillets,
weighing approximately 1 lb (450 g) when skinned
Pinch paprika

Prepare the sauce by combining all the ingredients in a large bowl and stirring to blend well.

Skin the chicken and cut into finger-sized strips. Add to the sauce and toss to coat thoroughly. Pile loosely into a serving bowl and dust with paprika.

Devilled Chicken Salad

Tender strips of poached or roasted chicken breast lightly coated in a mayonnaise flavoured with spices, garlic and herbs, served with slices of pear or melon and button mushrooms on a bed of mixed salad leaves. The more varied the leaves, the more intesting the salad.

SERVES 4

FOR THE DEVILLED SAUCE
1 egg yolk
5 fl oz (150 ml) olive or sunflower oil
1–2 tablespoons Worcestershire sauce
1 teaspoon tomato ketchup
1 tablespoon lemon juice
Pinch salt

FOR THE SALAD
4 chicken breasts, poached or roasted and cut into finger strips
A selection of salad leaves, washed and dried
2 pears or 1 wedge melon
4 oz (100 g) button mushrooms
Pinch paprika

First prepare the sauce by putting the egg yolk in a small bowl and gradually whisking in the oil to form a thick emulsion as if you were making mayonnaise. Stir in the remaining ingredients to give a hot spicy sauce.

Toss the prepared chicken strips in the sauce and arrange on the salad leaves. Peel, core and slice the pears or de-rind and slice the melon. Slice the mushrooms finely and sprinkle these on to the salad, then arrange the slices of pear or melon through the chicken. Finish with a dusting of paprika.

MEAT

CHILLI CON CARNE

A hot spicy minced-beef mixture with tomatoes, peppers and nutritious red kidney beans. For speed and convenience use a packet of commercially prepared chilli con carne mix and omit the tomato purée and seasonings. The method is the same and the result is excellent. Serve with white or brown rice.

SERVES 4

2 tablespoons sunflower oil
1 large onion, finely chopped
1 clove garlic, crushed
1 lb (450 g) lean minced beef
2 green peppers, de-seeded and diced
2 tablespoons tomato purée
½ teaspoon dried oregano
2 teaspoons chilli powder
Freshly ground black pepper
Pinch sugar
2 bay leaves
1 × 14 oz (397 g) tin plum tomatoes
15 fl oz (450 ml) beef stock
1 × 15¼ oz (432 g) tin red kidney beans, drained and rinsed

Heat the oil in a large saucepan and fry the onion and garlic until soft but not coloured. Stir in the beef and continue to fry until browned. Add the green peppers, tomato purée and seasonings. (If using a packet of chilli con carne mix, add this instead of the seasonings listed here.) Stir in the tinned tomatoes and their juice along with the beef stock and drained kidney beans. Bring to the boil, cover, reduce the heat and simmer gently for 30 minutes.

MINCED BEEF ROULADE

A savoury mince and vegetable mixture in a pastry package, quickly prepared and cooked in 45 minutes, this makes a perfect family meal. It's delicious hot with spicy tomato sauce (see p. 98) or cold with salad.

Frozen pastry, either home-made or bought, is a must for storing in the freezer. It can be defrosted in 30 minutes and quickly used for packages, toppings and tarts. When defrosting mince, however, it is best left overnight in the refrigerator and only used when completely defrosted.

SERVES 4

FOR THE SAVOURY FILLING
1 lb (450 g) lean minced beef
1 small onion, finely chopped
1 clove garlic, crushed
1 small carrot, grated
2 oz (50 g) white breadcrumbs
1 tablespoon tomato ketchup
1 tablespoon Worcestershire sauce
1 tablespoon finely chopped parsley
Pinch dried mixed herbs
Pinch salt
Freshly ground black pepper

FOR THE PASTRY
1 × 13 oz (368 g) packet frozen puff pastry, defrosted
1 small egg, beaten

Pre-heat the oven to gas mark 7, 425°F (220°C).

Combine the ingredients for the filling in a bowl and mix well. Form into a log shape approximately 3 × 10 inches (7.5 × 25 cm).

Roll the pastry thinly to a 12 inch (30 cm) square. Cut off a 2 inch (5 cm) strip from one side and reserve for decoration. Set the meat log along the long end of the pastry, brush the pastry edges with beaten egg and fold over the remaining pastry to form a neat package. Trim off the corners to give a neat curve and knock the pastry edges together with the back of a knife to seal. Flute the edge to decorate. Cut the reserved pastry strip into three and use each piece to form a diagonal lattice over the log, sticking it down with beaten egg. Set on a baking sheet, brush with more beaten egg to glaze and bake in the oven for approximately 45 minutes or until the pastry is risen and golden-brown, by which time the filling will be cooked. Serve cut in slices.

MEXICAN BEEF TACOS

Mexican taco shells, the perfect finger food, are fried and shaped tortillas – flat cakes made from stoneground wheat or maize flour. They are sold in boxes, have a long shelf-life which makes them ideal for the store-cupboard and are available from most good delicatessens and supermarkets. When warmed through, the tacos make wonderful containers for any variety of filling from a simple combination of left-over meats and seasonings to the traditional and purpose-made minced beef and bean mix flavoured with taco seasoning and topped with lettuce, tomatoes and olives. For convenience a tin of taco filling can be used.

SERVES 4

FOR THE FILLING
1 tablespoon sunflower oil
1 large onion, finely chopped
1 clove garlic, crushed
1 red pepper, de-seeded and chopped
1 lb (450 g) lean minced beef
1 packet taco seasoning or 2 teaspoons chilli powder
1 × 14 oz (397 g) tin plum tomatoes
1 × 15¼ oz (432 g) tin red kidney beans, drained and rinsed
Freshly ground black pepper

FOR THE TACO SHELLS
12 taco shells
*Shredded lettuce, chopped tomatoes, chopped cucumber, chopped green pepper
and a few black or green olives*

Pre-heat the oven to gas mark 4, 350°F (180°C).

Heat the oil in a large saucepan and fry the onion and garlic until soft but not coloured. Stir in the red pepper and beef and continue to fry until the meat has browned. Stir in the seasoning and fry for a minute to develop the flavour. Add the tomatoes and beans and bring to the boil. Season with pepper, reduce the heat and simmer, uncovered, for 20 minutes or until the flavours have blended and the meat is cooked through. The mixture should be rich and pulpy with very little liquid.

Place the taco shells on a baking sheet open end down: this will prevent them from closing while they are being heated. Warm through in the oven for 2–3 minutes.

Put a layer of the meat and bean mixture in the base of each shell, add a layer of crisp shredded lettuce, top with other chopped salad vegetables such as tomato, cucumber and peppers, and sprinkle over a few olives. Serve immediately.

MEATBALLS IN PIZZAIOLA SAUCE

Fried beef balls braised in a rich tomato and green pepper sauce. For convenience a jar or packet of commercially prepared tomato-based sauce can be used. It won't have quite the same texture but it is a speedy alternative. The recipe requires about 600 g (by weight) or 10 fl oz (300 ml) liquid measure. Meatballs in chilli sauce can be made by adding 1–2 teaspoons chilli sauce such as Tabasco to the pizzaiola sauce recipe. Serve either version of this dish with noodles or rice and a green salad.

SERVES 4

FOR THE MEATBALLS
1 egg
2 oz (50 g) coarse breadcrumbs
1 lb (450 g) lean minced beef
Small piece onion, grated
Freshly ground black pepper
Pinch salt
2 tablespoons plain flour
2 tablespoons sunflower oil

FOR THE PIZZAIOLA SAUCE

1 tablespoon sunflower oil
1 small onion, finely chopped
1 clove garlic, crushed
1 green pepper, de-seeded and chopped
1 × 14 oz (397 g) tin plum tomatoes
10 fl oz (300 ml) beef stock
2 tablespoons tomato ketchup
1 teaspoon dried basil
1 tablespoon finely chopped parsley
Pinch salt
Pinch sugar
Freshly ground black pepper
Finely chopped parsley, to garnish

Begin by making the meatballs. Break the egg into a large bowl, beat with a fork, then stir in the breadcrumbs. Add the minced beef, grated onion and seasoning and work together until well combined. You will find that your hand is the best piece of equipment for this job. Divide the mixture into 8 portions, shape each one into a ball and roll in a little flour. Heat 2 tablespoons sunflower oil and fry the meatballs until evenly brown, turning frequently. This will take about 10 minutes.

Meanwhile prepare the pizzaiola sauce. Heat 1 tablespoon sunflower oil in a saucepan and fry the onion and garlic until soft but not coloured. Add the green pepper and all the remaining ingredients except the parsley for garnishing and bring to the boil.

When the meatballs are well browned, transfer to the saucepan containing the sauce and cook gently on a medium heat for 30 minutes or until the meat is cooked through and the sauce rich, pulpy and slightly reduced. Garnish with chopped parsley and serve.

GREEK-STYLE MEATBALLS WITH YOGHURT AND MINT SAUCE

The basic ingredients for the meatballs in this recipe are similar to those served with pizzaiola sauce (p. 75); however, that's where the similarity ends. Greek-style meatballs are delicately flavoured with lemon and mint and are served with a cooling yoghurt, lemon and pine nut sauce – perfect for hot summer weather. Brown rice and a crisp leafy salad would go well with this dish.

SERVES 4

FOR THE MEATBALLS
1 egg
2 oz (50 g) coarse breadcrumbs
1 lb (450 g) lean minced beef
Small piece onion, grated
Freshly ground black pepper
1 tablespoon dried mint or 1 handful fresh mint leaves, finely chopped
Grated rind 1 lemon
2 tablespoons plain flour
2 tablespoons sunflower oil

FOR THE YOGHURT AND MINT SAUCE
9 fl oz (275 ml) Greek-style natural yoghurt
Juice 1 lemon
1 tablespoon pine nuts or other nuts as available, roughly chopped
1 teaspoon dried mint or 2 tablespoons finely chopped fresh mint
Freshly ground black pepper

Break the egg into a large bowl, beat with a fork, then stir in the breadcrumbs and leave to soak for about 5 minutes. Add the minced beef, grated onion, pepper, mint and lemon rind and work until well combined. Divide the mixture into 16 pieces about the size of a golf ball. Shape each piece into a ball and roll in a little flour. Fry in the sunflower oil until evenly brown and cooked through: this will take about 20 minutes.

Meanwhile make the sauce. Mix the yoghurt, lemon juice, pine (or other) nuts and mint together and set aside to allow the flavours to develop. Serve the meatballs with the yoghurt and mint sauce.

SPAGHETTI BOLOGNESE

The rich Italian meat sauce in this dish takes its name from its place of origin –
Bologna. It is generally served with spaghetti but also goes well with any other
type of pasta.

SERVES 4

FOR THE BOLOGNESE SAUCE
2 tablespoons sunflower oil
1 lb (450 g) lean minced beef
4 oz (100 g) bacon, finely diced
1 large onion, finely chopped
1 clove garlic, crushed
2 carrots, finely diced
1 tablespoon plain flour
3 tablespoons tomato purée
1 × 14 oz (397 g) tin plum tomatoes
15 fl oz (450 ml) beef stock
Freshly ground black pepper
Pinch salt
Pinch ground nutmeg
1 bay leaf
Grated Parmesan cheese, to serve

FOR THE PASTA
12 oz (350 g) spaghetti or other pasta
Pinch salt
Few drops sunflower oil
Melted butter
Freshly ground black pepper

To make the sauce, heat the oil in a heavy-based saucepan and fry the meat and
bacon until brown. Add the onion, garlic and carrots and continue to cook
until the onion is soft and slightly coloured. Stir in the flour and tomato purée,
blending well. Add all the remaining sauce ingredients (except for the Parmesan cheese), bring to the boil, cover, reduce the heat and simmer gently for
about 30 minutes.

To cook the pasta, place in a large pan of fast-boiling salted water to which a few drops of oil have been added to prevent it from sticking. When the water has returned to the boil, cook until the pasta is just slightly resistant or, as the Italians would say, '*al dente*'. This will take anything from 5 to 10 minutes depending on the type of pasta used: check the manufacturer's instruction. Drain when ready and toss in a little melted butter. Season with freshly ground pepper.

To serve, arrange the pasta around the edge of each of 4 plates and pour the meat sauce in the centre. Serve the Parmesan cheese separately.

CORNED BEEF AND CHEESE SAVOURY

Corned beef may not be to everyone's taste but it is a good store-cupboard standby and, combined with plum tomatoes and topped with mashed potatoes and cheese, it makes a very hearty meal for a hungry family. Serve on its own or with salad.

SERVES 4

1 × 7 oz (198 g) tin corned beef
1 × 7½ oz (213 g) tin plum tomatoes
Pinch salt
Freshly ground black pepper
1 egg, hard-boiled and sliced
4 oz (100 g) Cheddar cheese, grated
1 × 4½ oz (126 g) packet instant mashed potato mix

Pre-heat the oven to gas mark 6, 400°F (200°C).

Cut the corned beef into cubes and place in the bottom of a 2 pint (1.2 litre) ovenproof pie dish. Pour over the tinned tomatoes and their juice. Sprinkle with salt and pepper. Arrange the slices of hard-boiled egg on top and sprinkle with half the cheese. Make up the mashed potato according to the packet instructions and spread on top of the cheese. Rough the surface with a fork. Sprinkle with the remaining cheese and bake in the oven until very hot and crispy on top.

STIR-FRIED BEEF WITH VEGETABLES

Stir-fry dishes are so wonderfully quick to make that they are perfect for last-minute meals. Although this recipe combines fingers of beef with carrots, green pepper and mushrooms, other tender cuts of meat such as chicken or pork can be used along with whatever vegetables are available. The store-cupboard ingredients of soy sauce and pineapple will give the authentic sweet-and-sour Chinese taste. Serve the stir-fry with egg noodles or white rice.

SERVES 4

12 oz (350 g) quick-fry or rump steak
2 medium carrots
1 green pepper
4 oz (100 g) mushrooms
8 spring onions
3 tablespoons sunflower oil
1 clove garlic, sliced
1 tablespoon cornflour
3 tablespoons soy sauce
10 fl oz (300 ml) beef stock
1 × 13.5 oz (383 g) tin pineapple rings, cut into pieces, juice reserved

Cut the meat into thin finger strips. Cut the carrots into thin strips about 2½ × ⅛ inches (6 cm × 3 mm). Cut the pepper in half, discarding the seeds and pith, and cut into strips about 2½ × ¼ inches (6 cm × 5 mm). Thickly slice the mushrooms. Cut the spring onions into 2 inch (5 cm) lengths.

Heat the oil in a large frying-pan or wok, add the steak and carrots and stir-fry over a high heat for about 3 minutes, tossing them all the time. Add the green pepper, garlic, mushrooms and spring onions and stir-fry for a further 3 minutes.

Blend the cornflour with the soy sauce and gradually stir in the beef stock. Add to the pan along with the pineapple pieces and their juice. Bring to the boil, stirring and tossing continually. Cook for 1 minute. Serve immediately.

CURRIED BEEF AND ONION PATTIES

Beef and onion patties with a hint of Indian spice are quickly prepared from tinned corned beef, curry powder and mango chutney, making a useful store-cupboard meal. Serve hot with yoghurt and a crisp green salad.

SERVES 4

3 tablespoons sunflower oil
1 small onion, chopped
½ teaspoon curry powder or paste
1 × 2½ oz (65 g) packet instant mashed potato mix
2 tablespoons desiccated coconut
4 tablespoons milk
6 tablespoons water
1 × 7 oz (198 g) tin corned beef
1 tablespoon mango chutney
2 oz (50 g) white breadcrumbs
Freshly ground black pepper
1 egg, beaten
2 tablespoons plain flour

Heat 1 tablespoon of the sunflower oil in a frying-pan and fry the onion until soft and slightly coloured. Stir in the curry powder or paste and fry for a further few minutes to develop the flavour. Remove from the heat and leave to cool.

Empty the mashed potato mix into a bowl. Heat the desiccated coconut with the milk and water and pour on to the potato, stirring to reconstitute. Add the corned beef and fried onion. Mash with a fork to combine.

Stir in the mango chutney, breadcrumbs and pepper and bind with the beaten egg. Shape into 4 or 8 patties, using a little flour. Fry in the remaining 2 tablespoons hot oil until firm and golden, allowing about 5 minutes on each side, then serve.

MUSTARD LAMB CUTLETS

Lamb cutlets are among the faster, if slightly more expensive, fast foods but they do have a delicious taste, particularly when fried or grilled. Mustard cutlets, with their hot and crispy coat, are an interesting variation on a favourite dish. Serve with a crisp salad and baked potatoes.

SERVES 4

3 tablespoons English or French mustard
8 lamb cutlets, trimmed of excess fat
8 oz (250 g) dried fine white breadcrumbs
2 tablespoons demerara sugar
Freshly ground black pepper
1 egg

Spread the mustard thinly on each side of the cutlets. Mix the breadcrumbs, sugar and pepper together on a wide plate. Beat the egg on another plate until well blended. Dip the mustard-coated cutlets in the beaten egg and then in the crumb mixture, making sure they are evenly coated. Clean the cutlet bones and wrap in aluminium foil for protection.

If the cutlets are to be fried, use a large pan and about 3 tablespoons hot sunflower oil and fry over a moderate heat until the cutlets are cooked through and golden-brown. Allow about 5 minutes on each side.

If the cutlets are to be grilled, pre-heat the grill to a moderate heat and cook the cutlets, turning frequently until crisp and golden-brown on the outside and cooked through. This will take between 10 and 20 minutes.

PORK CHOPS WITH A CHEESY CRUST

Pork chops are a fast food which don't take up too much space in a small freezer, and which can be quickly defrosted and cooked when shopping time is limited and store-cupboard cookery is called for. This particular recipe braises the chops in a light stock which is then mixed with breadcrumbs and cheese to give a tasty topping. An excellent dish for entertaining when time is short served with vegetables of your choice.

SERVES 4

2 tablespoons sunflower oil
4 pork loin chops, trimmed of excess fat
1 large onion, finely chopped
5 fl oz (150 ml) dry white wine and 5 fl oz (150 ml) chicken stock
or 10 fl oz (300 ml) chicken stock
Freshly ground black pepper
4 tablespoons fresh white breadcrumbs
2 tablespoons finely chopped parsley
4 oz (100 g) Cheddar cheese, grated

Heat the oil in a large frying-pan and fry the chops until brown on both sides. Remove from the pan. Fry the onion in the remaining fat until soft but not coloured. Lay the chops on top of the cooked onions and pour on the wine (if using) and stock. Season with pepper. Bring the liquid to the boil, then reduce the heat to a simmer, cover and cook gently for about 20 minutes or until the pork is thoroughly cooked and tender.

Meanwhile combine the breadcrumbs, parsley and cheese in a bowl. When the chops are cooked, add a little of their liquid to the breadcrumbs and mix to a paste.

Transfer the chops and their sauce to a shallow ovenproof serving dish, spread the paste on top of the chops and brown under a hot grill. This will take about 3 minutes.

FRANKFURTER AND CHILLI BEAN POT

Frankfurters and beans are excellent partners and when combined with a hot chilli and tomato sauce make an interesting store-cupboard casserole. Serve with wholegrain rice (see p. 93). Frozen vegetarian frankfurters are now readily available from health-food stores and some supermarkets. They are of excellent quality and certainly worth trying.

SERVES 4

1 tablespoon sunflower oil
1 large onion, sliced
2 cloves garlic, crushed
1 teaspoon mild chilli powder
6 frankfurters
1 × 14 oz (397 g) tin plum tomatoes
1 × 15¼ oz (432 g) tin red kidney beans, drained and rinsed
5 fl oz (150 ml) vegetable stock
Freshly ground black pepper
2 tablespoons chopped parsley

Heat the oil in a large saucepan and fry the sliced onion and garlic until soft. Stir in the chilli powder and fry for 30 seconds to develop the flavour. Cut the frankfurters into 1½ inch (4 cm) lengths and add to the pot with the tomatoes, beans, stock and pepper. Bring to the boil, then reduce to a simmer. Cover and cook gently for 30–35 minutes until the flavours are well blended. If necessary, remove the lid for the final few minutes to reduce and thicken the sauce a little. Sprinkle with parsley and serve.

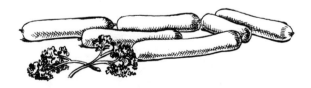

SAUSAGE STROGANOFF

A wonderfully quick and popular recipe which uses either best-quality low-fat sausages from a reputable butcher or the more convenient tinned frankfurter. Beware fatty sausages. Either way, this combination of sausage pieces, onions and mushrooms in a sour cream sauce is delicious. Accompany with pasta or rice.

SERVES 4

2 tablespoons sunflower oil
1 lb (450 g) best-quality low-fat beef sausages or 8 frankfurters
1 large onion, thinly sliced
4 oz (100 g) mushrooms, sliced
1 × 10¼ oz (295 g) tin condensed cream of mushroom soup
1 × 5 oz (142 g) carton sour cream or natural yoghurt
Freshly ground black pepper
2 tablespoons finely chopped parsley

If using fresh beef sausages, heat the oil in a large frying-pan and gently fry the sausages until brown and cooked thoroughly. This will take 8-10 minutes. Remove from the pan, cut diagonally into bite-size pieces and keep warm. If using frankfurters, boil in water for 5–10 minutes, then cut into pieces and keep warm.

Fry the onion until soft, then add the mushrooms and continue to fry until both are beginning to brown. Reserve a small quantity of onion, mushrooms and sausage pieces and keep warm. Add the remainder to the pan along with the soup. Stir well to combine. Bring to the boil, cook for a few minutes, then reduce the heat and stir in the sour cream or yoghurt. Season with pepper.

Serve topped with the reserved onion, mushrooms and sausages and a sprinkling of parsley.

PASTA AND RICE

PASTA AND A SELECTION OF SAUCES

Pasta is one of the store-cupboard cook's most valued assets because of its long shelf-life, its variety and the speed at which it can be cooked, not to mention its versatility. There is an incredibly wide range of both the dried and fresh varieties available in a rainbow of colours and flavours, and since most sorts of pasta cook very quickly, the sauce can be prepared and cooked at the same time. Dried pasta takes from 6–12 minutes to cook, depending on the type. Tagliatelle and fettucine usually take 6–8 minutes, the bows, shapes, spirals and macaroni 10 minutes and spaghetti 12 minutes. Wholewheat pasta needs longer and fresh pasta much less time – generally only 2–3 minutes. So keep testing until it is just tender. For a main course allow about 3 oz (75 g) dried pasta or 4 oz (100 g) fresh pasta per person; halve these amounts for a starter.

The secret of cooking pasta is to use a large saucepan three-quarters full of water to which 1 teaspoon salt and a few drops of oil have been added and cook at a fast rolling boil without the lid. Once the pasta has been added to the pan, return to the boil before timing. Indeed, the cooking procedure is the same as for rice. Drain the pasta well, then toss in a little oil or melted butter to prevent sticking and add your favourite sauce. Here are several quick ones to try. Each recipe serves 4 people as a main course.

ANCHOVY, OLIVE AND TOMATO SAUCE

Specially for those who enjoy the true taste of the Mediterranean. Put 2×2 oz (50 g) tins anchovies together with their oil in a saucepan with 2 crushed cloves garlic and 1 tablespoon sunflower oil and cook over a gentle heat, stirring the anchovies until they form a paste with the oil. Stir in a pinch of chilli powder, 16 stoned black olives, ½ tablespoon each dried oregano and basil and 1×14 oz (397 g) tin plum tomatoes. Simmer over a low heat for about 10 minutes until thick, pulpy and well blended. Pour over the hot pasta and toss.

ONION, BACON AND TOMATO SAUCE

Fry 1 finely chopped onion and 1 clove garlic in 2 tablespoons sunflower oil until soft. Add 6 oz (175 g) diced lean bacon and continue to fry until cooked and lightly browned. Stir in 1 × 7½ oz (213 g) tin plum tomatoes or 4–6 chopped fresh tomatoes along with 1 tablespoon finely chopped parsley. Cook for a few minutes to combine. Season with freshly ground black pepper and add to the hot pasta.

MUSSEL, MUSHROOM AND MUSTARD SAUCE

Fry 1 finely chopped onion and 2 cloves garlic in 2 tablespoons sunflower oil until soft. Stir in 6 oz (175 g) sliced mushrooms and continue to fry until beginning to brown. Add 1 × 4 oz (105 g) tin smoked mussels together with their oil along with 5 fl oz (150 ml) cream blended with 2 tablespoons Dijon mustard. Stir carefully to combine without breaking the mussels. Cook gently for 2–3 minutes. Season with freshly ground black pepper, a squeeze of lemon juice and 2 tablespoons chopped parsley. Toss with the hot pasta and serve.

BACON, MUSHROOM AND CHEESE SAUCE

Fry 1 crushed clove garlic with 4 oz (100 g) bacon cut into small pieces, 4 oz (100 g) sliced mushrooms and a pinch each of dried oregano and basil in about 1 tablespoon hot sunflower oil until slightly browned. Sprinkle on 2 oz (50 g) grated Parmesan or Cheddar cheese and 10 fl oz (300 ml) cream. Stir all the time until the sauce thickens but taking care it doesn't boil. Season with freshly ground black pepper and if necessary adjust the consistency with a little milk. Pour on to the hot pasta and serve with extra grated Parmesan cheese.

CREAM AND CHEESE SAUCE

One of the simplest sauces possible but perhaps not for the health-conscious! Beat 2 egg yolks with 5 fl oz (150 ml) single cream and stir in 2–4 oz (50–100 g) grated Parmesan or Cheddar cheese. Add to the hot pasta and toss for a few minutes over a low heat until the cheese has melted and the sauce is thick and warm. Serve with freshly ground black pepper and extra grated Parmesan cheese.

SAUCY BOTTLES

There are a number of ready-made bottled and tinned sauces now widely available in supermarkets and delicatessens, some of which are well worth trying with pasta. Two of the best are the bottled tomato sauces and the Italian pesto sauce, which is made from fresh basil, garlic, olive oil and pine nuts. The tomato sauces are good value but the pesto, because of its ingredients, is more expensive. For this reason I extend it by adding 2 fl oz (50 ml) sunflower oil and 4 tablespoons hot water per 3¼ fl oz (106 ml) jar pesto sauce. This is then added to the hot pasta and served with freshly ground black pepper and grated Parmesan cheese.

The spicy tomato sauce recipe on page 98 is also excellent with pasta and quick to make. Just reduce it until it is of a thick pulpy consistency, mix with lots of chopped parsley and pour on the hot pasta. Serve with grated Parmesan cheese.

A short-cut on sauces is to use a well-flavoured soft cream cheese such as garlic and herb. Gently heat 1 × 5 oz (150 g) packet or piece of cheese in a saucepan with 1 tablespoon cream or milk until the cheese has melted. Then toss with the hot pasta and finish with freshly ground black pepper and some grated Parmesan.

The use of cream in pasta sauces, although very rich, is hard to beat for both flavour and texture. Fromage frais can be used instead but the consistency and texture are not as good. Yoghurt, although more healthy, gives a very poor, thin, gritty result. If you cannot or do not wish to use cream, go for one of the vegetable or fish-based sauces.

TAGLIATELLE WITH SALMON AND MUSHROOMS

Tagliatelle, the most common form of flat ribbon noodles, are available both loose and in nests, in plain, wholewheat or spinach flavour. Here they are combined with a rich sauce of salmon, mushrooms and tomato with a hint of the Italian herb oregano, and topped with cheese before being baked in the oven: a truly delicious dish for family and friends. Serve with a tossed salad and fresh crusty bread.

SERVES 4

FOR THE TAGLIATELLE
6 oz (175 g) plain tagliatelle
Salt
Dash sunflower oil
3 large tomatoes, chopped
2 tablespoons tomato purée

FOR THE MUSHROOM AND SALMON SAUCE
1 tablespoon sunflower oil
1 large onion, finely chopped
1 clove garlic, crushed
6 oz (175 g) mushrooms, sliced
2 teaspoons dried oregano
1 × 7½ oz (213 g) tin salmon in oil, drained and flaked
1 oz (25 g) sunflower margarine
1 oz (25 g) plain flour
1 pint (600 ml) milk
Salt and freshly ground black pepper
Squeeze lemon juice
4 oz (100 g) Cheddar cheese, grated

Pre-heat the oven to gas mark 5, 375°F (190°C).

Cook the tagliatelle in a large pan of boiling, salted and oiled water (see p. 85) until just cooked or *al dente*. This will take about 6–8 minutes. Drain the pasta and refresh under cold running water until cold. Set aside while preparing the sauce.

Heat the sunflower oil in a large frying-pan and fry the onion, garlic and mushrooms until just beginning to colour. Stir in the oregano and salmon. Remove from the heat.

Melt the sunflower margarine in a saucepan, stir in the flour and cook on a low heat for a few minutes. Remove from the heat and gradually add the milk, stirring all the time to prevent lumps from forming. Return to the heat, bring to the boil and cook until thickening. Season well with salt, pepper and lemon juice. Pour over the mushroom mixture.

Everything is now ready to combine for baking. Lightly oil a 3 pint (1.75 litre) ovenproof dish approximately 2 inches (5 cm) deep. Place half the tagliatelle in the bottom. Spread the tomatoes and tomato purée on top and cover with half the mushroom and salmon sauce. Lay the rest of the pasta on top, followed by the remaining sauce. Cover with grated cheese and bake in the oven for 25–30 minutes or until bubbling and golden-brown.

SPAGHETTI ALLA CARBONARA

One of the most popular and tasty of the pasta dishes and again an excellent store-cupboard standby. Sliced ham, salami, or lightly fried fingers of liver could be used instead of the bacon.

SERVES 4

FOR THE SPAGHETTI
12 oz (350 g) spaghetti
Large pinch salt
Dash sunflower oil

FOR THE CARBONARA SAUCE
1 tablespoon sunflower oil
1 small onion, finely chopped
1 clove garlic, crushed
8 oz (225 g) lean bacon, cut into thin strips
4 eggs
1 × 5 fl oz (150 ml) carton single or double cream
2 oz (50 g) Parmesan cheese, grated, plus extra for serving
Freshly ground black pepper

Cook the spaghetti until tender in a large pan of boiling water to which salt and a few drops of oil have been added (see p. 85). It will take about 12 minutes.

While the spaghetti is cooking, make the carbonara sauce. Heat the oil in a frying-pan and fry the onion, garlic and bacon until the onion is soft and just beginning to colour. This will take about 5–8 minutes. Beat the eggs in a bowl and stir in the cream and 2 oz (50 g) cheese and season with pepper.

Drain the pasta well, return to the hot pan and pour on the egg and cheese liquid. Toss over a gentle heat to combine and cook the sauce. Stir in the hot bacon mixture with its juices and serve with extra Parmesan and more pepper.

NOODLE AUFLAUF

This delicious pasta dish from Switzerland, perfect for family lunch or supper, combines tagliatelle with cooked ham baked in a savoury egg custard – most unusual but quick and tasty. Serve with a crisp, green salad.

SERVES 4

9 oz (250 g) plain or spinach tagliatelle
Salt
Dash sunflower oil
4–6 oz (100–175 g) cooked ham, roughly chopped or cut into strips
3–4 eggs
10 fl oz (300 ml) milk
Pinch salt
Freshly ground black pepper
3–4 oz (75–100 g) Cheddar cheese, grated

Pre-heat the oven to gas mark 5, 375°F (190°C).

Cook the tagliatelle in boiling, salted and oiled water (see p. 85) until just tender or al dente. This will take about 6–8 minutes. Drain and put with the cooked ham in an ovenproof dish of approximately 2½ pints (1.5 litres) capacity and 2 inches (5 cm) deep. Mix the eggs with the milk, season with salt and pepper and pour over the ham and noodles. If the noodles are not completely covered, add more milk. Sprinkle with the grated cheese and bake in the oven for approximately 25–30 minutes or until the custard is soft set and the cheese golden-brown.

90S MACARONI CHEESE

A delicious and economical savoury dish from the past, perfect for lunch, high tea or supper. Traditionally it combines some basic ingredients from the store-cupboard – macaroni, bacon, eggs and tomato in a well-flavoured cheese sauce – but it can just as easily be made with other ingredients. A 7 oz (200 g) tin of tuna fish could replace the bacon and the seasoning could include 2 table-spoons of chopped parsley and a squeeze of lemon juice. For a vegetarian alter-native replace the bacon with 8 oz (225 g) of cooked vegetables and add a few herbs and spices. The results will all be very different, but certainly worth try-ing! Serve with salad and pickled gherkins.

SERVES 4

FOR THE MACARONI MIXTURE
6 oz (175 g) short-cut macaroni
Salt
Dash sunflower oil
1 small onion, chopped and lightly fried
6–8 oz (175 –225 g) lean bacon, cubed and fried
2 eggs, hard-boiled and sliced
4 tomatoes, sliced

FOR THE CHEESE SAUCE
1 pint (600 ml) milk
Piece onion
1 blade mace
1 bay leaf
2 oz (50 g) sunflower margarine
2 oz (50 g) plain flour
Pinch salt
Freshly ground black pepper
2 teaspoons English mustard
4 oz (100 g) Cheddar cheese, grated

Pre-heat the oven to gas mark 6, 400°F (200°C).

Begin by cooking the macaroni in a large saucepan of boiling water to which some salt and a little oil have been added (see p. 85). Cook for about 10 min-utes or until just tender.

While the macaroni is cooking, prepare the cheese sauce. Warm the milk with the onion, mace and bay leaf. Remove from the heat and leave to infuse for 5 minutes. Melt the margarine in a saucepan, stir in the flour and cook gently for a few minutes. Remove from the heat. Strain the milk and gradually add to the margarine and flour mixture, stirring constantly to prevent lumps from forming. Return the saucepan to the heat, season with salt, pepper, mustard and two-thirds of the cheese and keep warm.

Drain the pasta and add to the cheese sauce along with the onion and cooked bacon. Stir to combine. Pour half of this mixture into an ovenproof serving dish about 2 inches (5 cm) deep and 3 pints (1.75 litres) in capacity. Arrange the sliced hard-boiled egg on top. Cover with the rest of the macaroni. Arrange the tomato slices over the surface and sprinkle with the remaining cheese. Place on a baking sheet and bake in the oven for 20–30 minutes or until bubbling hot and crisp and brown on top.

LONG-GRAIN WHITE AND BROWN RICE

There are many different ways to cook long-grain rice and cooks will eventually find one which gives them the most satisfactory end product. For me the following method never fails to produce the dry fluffy result that I like. If you've had difficulty cooking rice and constantly end up with a sticky gelatinous substance, try this method and you should have no more problems – provided you follow the recipe carefully!

Allow 2 oz (50 g) long-grain rice per person for a main course, and ½–1 oz (15–25 g) per person if the rice is to be an accompaniment to a selection of main-course dishes on a buffet table where a potato or pasta dish is also served.

Rice needs lots of room to bounce around in the saucepan so that the grains can cook individually and not stick together in a mass; therefore, no matter how small the quantity of rice to be cooked, choose a large saucepan. It is advisable not to cook more than 1 lb (450 g) rice in 5 pints (2.75 litres) water, otherwise the results could be disappointing.

Now to the cooking: three-quarters fill a large saucepan with water and bring to the boil. Add 1 tablespoon salt and a good squeeze of lemon juice. When the water is boiling fast, add the rice, stir once to make sure that no grains stick to the bottom of the pan and allow to return to the boil. Note the time once boiling point is reached and cook with the lid off for 11 minutes exactly if preparing white rice; the water should boil fast throughout the cooking time. When the cooking time is up, test the rice by biting into a grain: it should be tender but still have a 'bite' to it. If it seems to be too hard, cook for a further 1 minute only, then test again: this should be all the time needed. If the rice is cooked too long, it will become very soft and mushy.

Drain the rice in a sieve, then rinse in boiling water to wash away any excess starch. Return the rice to the saucepan, cover with a piece of kitchen paper and dry over a low heat for a few minutes, shaking the pan to prevent the rice from sticking. This will remove any excess moisture in the rice and keep each grain loose and separate. If you aren't going to use the rice immediately, turn it into a buttered shallow serving dish, make a few air holes through the rice using the handle of a wooden spoon and cover with buttered foil. Place in the oven at gas mark 4, 350°F (180°C), for approximately 15 minutes. Remove the foil, fork up the rice so that it looks fluffy and loose, and serve.

Long-grain brown rice Cooks in exactly the same way but will take longer, anything from 25–40 minutes depending on the brand.

PREPARING RICE FOR A SALAD

Cold rice salads are very popular as part of a cold buffet table and not only taste good but can look very attractive too. For the busy host or hostess a cold rice salad is a great help because it can be prepared a day in advance and only requires the final touches a few hours before it's needed.

Cook the rice as described above then, after rinsing in boiling water, rinse again under cold running water until it is completely cold. Gently lift your fingers through the grains to ensure that the water circulates and that the rice cools as quickly as possible. Once cold, drain well and spread in a shallow layer on a tray covered with kitchen paper: the aim is to enable each grain to drain and dry properly. Cover loosely with another piece of kitchen paper and leave in a cold place until needed (overnight is fine). Just before serving, carefully brush the grains of rice off the kitchen paper into a bowl large enough to allow easy mixing of the rice and any other ingredients in the recipe; if the rice is to be served plain, turn directly into a serving dish, making sure that the grains are not flattened or packed tightly together. The rice should be loose and light, not compressed and heavy.

BEANS AND THINGS

RED-HOT BEAN CASSEROLE

A rich vegetable stew, spiced with chilli pepper and coloured with the vegetables of your choice – red and green peppers always add a sparkle to this dish, along with a delicate sweetness, and red kidney beans and bulgur wheat enrich and thicken the tomato sauce. Serve with a crunchy green salad and garlic and herb bread (see p. 95).

SERVES 4

2 tablespoons sunflower oil
1 large onion, finely chopped
1 clove garlic, crushed
1 lb (450 g) mixed vegetables (such as carrot, celery, parsnip and red and green peppers), chopped
1 teaspoon chilli powder
½ teaspoon dried basil
2 tablespoons finely chopped parsley
1 tablespoon red wine vinegar
2 tablespoons tomato purée
1 × 14 oz (397 g) tin plum tomatoes
1 pint (600 ml) vegetable stock
2 oz (50 g) bulgur wheat
1 × 15¼ oz (432 g) tin red kidney beans, drained and rinsed
Freshly ground black pepper

Heat the oil in a large saucepan or flameproof casserole and gently fry the onion and garlic until soft but not coloured. Add the remainder of the vegetables and continue to cook for a few minutes. Stir in the rest of the ingredients. Bring to the boil, then reduce the heat, cover and simmer for 30 minutes or until the vegetables are cooked.

GARLIC AND HERB BREAD

SERVES 4-6
---

4 oz (100 g) sunflower margarine
3 tablespoons fresh parsley, finely chopped
1 teaspoon mixed dried herbs or 2 teaspoons mixed fresh herbs
Juice ¼ lemon
2–4 cloves garlic, peeled and crushed
Freshly milled black pepper
1 French stick

Pre-heat the oven to gas mark 7, 425°F (220°C). Beat the margarine with the herbs, lemon juice, garlic and seasoning. Cut the French stick in half lengthwise but leave it attached along one side. Spread the herb and garlic butter along the inside of the bread and close to seal the cut edges together. Cut 1 in (2.5 cm) diagonal slices through the stick along its length. Carefully transfer to a sheet of aluminium foil and roll up tightly to keep in shape. Bake for 10–15 minutes in the oven. To serve, remove the bread from the foil and pile on a serving plate or bread basket.

BRETON BEANS

A delicious and nutritious mixture of white beans, tomatoes and onions, good hot or cold. Serve on its own with crusty bread or as an accompaniment to roast leg of lamb.

SERVES 4

2 tablespoons sunflower oil
2 onions, finely sliced
2 cloves garlic, crushed
2 × 14 oz (397 g) tins plum tomatoes
1 tablespoon dried basil
2½ fl oz (65 ml) vegetable stock or white wine
1 bay leaf
1 teaspoon sugar
Freshly ground black pepper
2 × 15¼ oz (430 g) tins butter beans, drained and rinsed
1 tablespoon chopped parsley, plus extra to garnish

Heat the oil in a large saucepan and fry the onions and garlic until soft but not coloured. Stir in the remainder of the ingredients, bring to the boil, then reduce the heat. Cover and simmer until the tomatoes are thick and pulpy and the flavours are well blended. This will take about 30–35 minutes. Adjust the seasoning, sprinkle with a little chopped parsley and serve. The flavour will become more intense if this dish is prepared the day before serving.

Mixed Nut Savoury

A wonderful combination of nuts – hazelnuts, peanuts, walnuts, pecans, Brazils, or whatever you have in your store-cupboard – mixed with wholemeal bread, herbs and stock to produce a most satisfying, nutritious and versatile dish. This basic recipe can be made into a savoury loaf or individual rissoles or burgers and is excellent served with spicy tomato sauce (p. 98) and green salad.

SERVES 4

1 tablespoon sunflower oil
1 onion, finely chopped
8 oz (225 g) mixed nuts
4 oz (100 g) wholemeal bread
1 teaspoon dried marjoram
2 tablespoons finely chopped parsley
Freshly ground black pepper
Pinch salt (optional)
1 egg made up to 5 fl oz (150 ml) with vegetable stock

Heat the oil in a frying-pan and fry the onion until soft and slightly coloured. Grind the nuts and bread together until quite fine but not powdered. A liquidiser, food processor, coffee grinder or nut mill can be used for this.

Combine the nut and bread mixture with the onion in a large bowl. Add the herbs and seasoning. Mix well. Stir in the egg and stock to bind the ingredients.

This savoury mixture can now be used to make one of the following:

Nut Roast

Pre-heat the oven to gas mark 4, 350°F (180°C).

Line a 1 lb (450 g) loaf tin with foil and oil lightly. Turn the savoury nut mixture into the prepared tin, pressing it down well to make sure there are no air spaces. Cover with a piece of lightly oiled foil, set on a baking sheet and bake in the oven for about 40 minutes or until firm to the touch.

Allow to cool slightly before turning out and removing the foil. Serve cut in 12–14 slices with a spicy tomato sauce (see p. 98). Allow 2–3 slices per person. This can be served hot or cold – and it's very filling.

NUT RISSOLES OR BURGERS

Divide the mixed nut savoury into 4 or 8 round cakes. Coat with finely ground wholemeal breadcrumbs and fry in a little hot sunflower oil until golden-brown and completely warmed through. This will take about 3–5 minutes on each side over a gentle heat. Serve hot or cold with spicy tomato sauce (see below).

SPICY TOMATO SAUCE

A thick well-flavoured tomato sauce, quick to make and delicious with meat, fish, vegetables, nut roast, burgers or pasta. In fact it's one of the most valuable recipes in the collection because it can transform even the simplest dish into a sophisticated creation. This freezes beautifully either in large or small quantities and is an excellent addition to the freezer store.

MAKES 16 FL OZ (475 ML) SAUCE
SERVES 4

1 tablespoon sunflower oil
1 medium onion, finely chopped
1–2 cloves garlic, crushed
1 × 14 oz (397 g) tin plum tomatoes
2½ fl oz (65 ml) vegetable stock
1 teaspoon sugar
Pinch dried basil
Pinch salt
Pinch ground cinnamon
Freshly ground black pepper

Heat the oil in a saucepan and fry the onion and garlic until soft but not coloured. Add the rest of the ingredients. Bring to the boil, then reduce the heat, cover and simmer for 20 minutes to reduce the liquid and concentrate the flavours.

The sauce can be served just as it is, thick and pulpy, or liquidised to give a smooth finish.

MUSHROOM RISOTTO

Risotto is one of the most versatile dishes that you could prepare and it can be as cheap or as expensive as you like, depending on the ingredients you choose to combine with the rice. Although all the ingredients will probably be in the store-cupboard or refrigerator, and it is easily and relatively quickly prepared, this Italian dish is not one that can be left to its own devices. It needs to be stood over, stirred and loved until it becomes moist, sticky and the rice is just tender. It really is worth the effort. Young spring vegetables such as baby carrots, courgettes, leeks and celery are perfect cut in ¾ inch (2 cm) cubes and added without previous cooking, as are peas and beans.

SERVES 4

2 oz (50 g) butter or sunflower margarine
1 small onion, finely chopped
8 oz (225 g) mushrooms, thickly sliced
7 oz (200 g) long- or short-grain white rice (see p. 19)
1 pint (600 ml) warm vegetable or chicken stock
2 fl oz (50 ml) dry white wine (optional)
Knob butter (optional)
Pinch salt
Freshly ground black pepper
Freshly grated Parmesan cheese

Melt the butter or margarine in a large frying-pan and gently fry the onion until soft. Add the mushrooms and fry for a further minute without colouring. Stir the rice into the onion and mushroom mixture and toss to coat in the fat. Do not let the contents of the pan brown. Add about 5 fl oz (150 ml) of the warm stock and continue to stir until absorbed. The rice will immediately start to become creamy. Continue adding the stock in this way, a little at a time, stirring continuously, until the rice is almost cooked. It should be sticky and shiny on the outside but still have a slight 'bite' in the middle. This will take about 15–20 minutes.

Just before the rice is cooked add the wine and knob of butter (if using) and season to taste. Serve immediately with freshly grated Parmesan cheese.

BULGUR WHEAT RISOTTO

This partially cooked wheat, sometimes known as cracked wheat, burghul wheat or pourgouri, is not only one of the quickest grains to cook, but has a lovely, nutty flavour too. It is excellent for risottos or pilaus. I have used the coarse bulgur which has a slightly rough texture but any texture of bulgur is fine.

SERVES 4

8 oz (225 g) bulgur wheat
2 tablespoons sunflower or nut oil
1 large onion, finely chopped
6 oz (175 g) mushrooms, sliced and fried
4 oz (100 g) whole hazel or other nuts
1 pint (600 ml) vegetable stock
2 tablespoons soy sauce
3 tablespoons finely chopped parsley
6 oz (175 g) peas, sweetcorn kernels or courgettes, or a mixture of all 3
Freshly ground black pepper

Rinse the bulgur wheat in a fine-meshed sieve under cold running water. Leave to drain. Heat the oil in a large saucepan and gently fry the onion, mushrooms and nuts for about 8 minutes with the lid on the pan to draw out the flavours. Add the bulgur wheat, stock, soy sauce and 2 tablespoons of the chopped parsley. Bring to the boil, then reduce the heat, cover and simmer gently for about 10 minutes or until the wheat is almost tender.

Add the vegetables and cook for a further 3–5 minutes. Season to taste with black pepper and serve sprinkled with the remaining 1 tablespoon parsley.

TASTY TOASTIES

No matter how empty the fridge, freezer or store-cupboard may be, there are generally a few items which, with a little imagination, can be turned into a quick tasty snack. Bread, a staple food in most diets and one which the store-cupboard is rarely without, either fresh or frozen, is the ideal base for these efforts, and certainly nowadays there is no shortage of variety. Crisp whites, nutty browns, rolls of all shapes, sizes and grains and a vast array of international breads, including French sticks, Italian pizza bases and Lebanese pitta bread, ensure that there's something for everyone. Whether it be a traditional toasted sandwich, a base with a savoury topping or a stuffed pocket of pitta bread, anything from a simple poached egg on toast to an elegant smoked salmon rarebit will go.

SCRAMBLED SAVOURY

Flavour a scrambled egg with mixed herbs, chopped ham, tomatoes and onion and serve on a toasted bap with a garnish of salad leaves, or use to fill a pitta bread pouch.

BACON AND MUSHROOM TOAST

Fry some chopped bacon with finely sliced mushrooms in a little sunflower oil until cooked and beginning to brown, stir in a few tablespoons of cream or yoghurt and pile on a piece of hot toast.

SALMON SAVOURY

Combine 1×7 oz (200 g) tin salmon (drained) in a bowl with 1 oz (25 g) grated cheese, 2 tablespoons natural yoghurt, some freshly ground black pepper, a few chopped gherkins (optional) and 1 tablespoon finely chopped parsley. Lightly toast a slice of bread on both sides, pile the filling on top and sprinkle with a little more grated cheese. Grill until the cheese is melted and bubbling and the salmon mixture heated through.

CROQUE MONSIEUR

Make a sandwich with buttered bread and a filling of grated cheese and sliced ham. Cut the crusts off the bread and cut each sandwich into three fingers. Fry the sandwiches in butter until golden and crisp on both sides. Serve at once with a crisp side salad. Chopped mushrooms, sardines, salmon or any other ingredient of your choice can be mixed with the cheese to vary the filling.

FRENCH TOAST

Beat a large egg on a shallow plate, lay a slice of bread in it and leave to soak for a few minutes. Meanwhile, heat a knob of butter (or a little sunflower oil) in a large frying-pan and fry the soaked bread until puffy and golden brown on both sides. Serve either sweet sprinkled with sugar and cinnamon or savoury with fried rashers of bacon and tomatoes.

WELSH RAREBIT

Put 3 oz (75 g) cheese, ½ oz (15 g) butter, a pinch of English mustard powder, 2 tablespoons beer and a pinch each of salt and freshly ground black pepper in a saucepan and heat very slowly over a low heat, stirring occasionally, until the mixture is smooth and creamy. Spoon the cheese mixture on to a slice of lightly toasted bread and place under a hot grill until golden and bubbling. Serve at once with grilled tomatoes, rashers of bacon and a green salad. For Buck rarebit, top with a poached egg.

PIZZA BAPS

For this instant pizza use a large bap, a soft roll, or a piece of French bread cut in half. Chop a slice of salami (rind removed) and arrange on the top of the bread. Cover with sliced or chopped tomatoes and sliced Cheddar cheese, and top with a few olives and anchovy fillets if liked. Sprinkle with dried basil, oregano or marjoram and cook under a hot grill until the cheese is bubbling and golden. Serve hot with salad or cold for a packed lunch.

PITTA BREAD POCKETS

These make wonderful containers for a great variety of fillings. Grill the pitta bread first. Slide a knife horizontally into the toasted pitta, open it up to make a pocket and stuff with a filling of your choice. Try chicken and apple salad: combine pieces of shredded cooked chicken with chopped celery and apple, moisten with a little mayonnaise to bind; line the pitta pockets with shredded lettuce and fill with the chicken salad. Scrambled savoury (p. 101) and chicken koftas (p. 64) also make tasty and substantial fillings for pitta bread pockets.

VEGETABLES

POTATO CAKES

Potato cake, also called potato bread or fadge, is a traditional Irish dish served hot with butter and sugar or fried and eaten with bacon, sausages and eggs as part of a concoction called 'Irish fry', which is served for breakfast, lunch or tea.

Potato cake is best made while the potatoes are still hot. If using left-over potato, heat for 30 seconds in the microwave. However you heat it, it must be warmed through just enough to keep it from being stodgy.

SERVES 4

8 oz (225 g) potatoes, cooked
½ teaspoon salt
1 oz (25 g) butter or sunflower margarine, melted
2 oz (50 g) plain flour

Put the potatoes through a potato ricer or mash well until smooth and free from lumps. Add the salt and melted butter, then work in enough flour to make a pliable dough.

Roll into a circle about ¼ inch (5 mm) thick and 9 inches (23 cm) in dia-meter. Cut into 6 or 8 triangle shapes (farls), or 10 rounds using a 3 inch (7.5 cm) cutter, and bake on a hot griddle or cook in a frying-pan until lightly browned on both sides. This will take about 5 minutes. Don't use oil in the pan, but test to see if it's hot enough by sprinkling a little flour over the base: when it turns golden, the pan is ready.

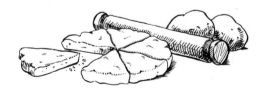

STUFFED POTATO PILLOWS

Double the quantity of potato cake dough given in the previous recipe to make 12 pillows, allowing 3 for each serving.

SERVES 4

2 quantities potato cake dough (see p. 103)

FOR THE BACON, ONION AND MUSHROOM FILLING
2 tablespoons sunflower oil
2 rashers back bacon, rinded and diced
2 tablespoons finely chopped onion
4 oz (100 g) mushrooms, finely chopped or sliced
Freshly ground black pepper

FOR THE TOMATO AND PEPPER FILLING
1 tablespoon sunflower oil
1 small onion, finely chopped
1 clove garlic, crushed
1 small red or green pepper, de-seeded and finely chopped
1 tomato, finely chopped
Freshly ground black pepper
Pinch each paprika and salt

To make the bacon, onion and mushroom filling, heat the oil in a frying-pan and fry the bacon and onion until beginning to colour. Add the mushrooms and cook for a few minutes more. Season with pepper and allow to cool before using to fill the potato pillows.

To make the tomato and pepper filling, heat the oil in a frying-pan and fry the onion, garlic and pepper until soft. Add the tomato and seasoning and continue to fry for a few minutes. Allow to cool before using to fill the pillows.

Prepare the potato cake dough as described on p. 103 but roll out slightly thinner and cut into 24 circles using a 3 inch (7.5 cm) cutter. Moisten the edges of 12 of the circles with a little milk or water, then divide the filling of your choice between the 12 leaving a small rim around the edges. Use the remaining 12 circles as lids to cover the filling and press the edges together to seal. Cook on a pre-heated griddle or in a frying-pan over a low heat until brown on both sides and warm through. This will take about 8–10 minutes.

VEGETABLE GOULASH WITH TOPPINGS

A spicy and versatile stew, equally delicious on its own or with one of the top-pings suggested below. Breadcrumbs and cheese give a crisp crunchy finish, wholemeal flour and oats make a crumbly topping, and savoury scones baked on the surface of the stew produce a very substantial dish – indeed, a complete meal in a pot!

SERVES 4

2 tablespoons sunflower oil
1 medium onion, finely chopped
1 large courgette
2 carrots
1 parsnip
2 sticks celery
1¼ lb (500 g) potatoes
1 tablespoon paprika
½ teaspoon caraway seeds
1 tablespoon dried basil
1 × 14 oz (397 g) tin plum tomatoes
15 fl oz (450 ml) vegetable stock
Freshly ground black pepper
5 fl oz (150 ml) natural yoghurt
4 tablespoons finely chopped parsley

Heat the oil in a large flameproof casserole and fry the onion until soft but not coloured. Cut the vegetables into ½–1 inch (1–2.5 cm) cubes. Add the vege-tables to the casserole. Stir in all the remaining ingredients except the yoghurt and 2 tablespoons of the parsley, bring to the boil, then reduce the heat and simmer until the vegetables are tender. This will take about 20–30 minutes. Adjust the seasoning, stir in the yoghurt, sprinkle with the remaining 2 table-spoons parsley and serve; alternatively, top with one of the mixtures on the following page.

WHOLEMEAL BREAD AND CHEESE TOPPING

5 oz (150 g) wholemeal breadcrumbs
4 oz (100 g) Cheddar cheese, grated

Mix the breadcrumbs and cheese together and sprinkle over the top of the cooked goulash. Brown under a pre-heated grill until the cheese is bubbling and the topping golden-brown in colour.

CRUMBLE TOPPING

2 oz (50 g) block vegetable margarine
5 oz (150 g) plain wholemeal flour
1 oz (25 g) porridge oats
2–4 oz (50–100 g) Cheddar cheese, grated (optional)

Pre-heat the oven to gas mark 6, 400°F (200°C).

Rub the fat into the flour until the mixture resembles fine breadcrumbs. Stir in the oats and spread on top of the goulash about half-way through its cooking time. Sprinkle the grated cheese over this, if using. Cook for a further 30–40 minutes in the oven until the crumble is crisp and crunchy on the top (or golden-brown if topped with cheese).

SAVOURY SCONE TOPPING

12 oz (350 g) plain flour
2 tablespoons cream of tartar
1 tablespoon bicarbonate of soda
1 teaspoon salt
2 oz (50 g) block vegetable margarine
8 fl oz (250 ml) milk
4 oz (100 g) Cheddar cheese, grated (optional)

Pre-heat the oven to gas mark 7, 425°F (220°C).

Sift the dry ingredients into a large bowl. Cut and rub in the margarine until the mixture resembles fine breadcrumbs. Make a well in the centre and pour in all the milk. Stir to form a dough.

Turn on to a floured work-surface and knead lightly. Roll out to ½–1 inch (1–2.5 cm) thick and cut into scones using a 2½ inch (6 cm) plain cutter.

Arrange the scones on top of the goulash about half-way through its cooking time, sprinkle the cheese over them (if using) and bake in the oven for 25 minutes until the scones are risen and golden in colour.

STIR-FRIED GREEN VEGETABLES

Stir-frying is the best way of cooking vegetables to retain their colour, crispness and much of their food value. Choose a selection of vegetables according to the season and what is available in the store-cupboard and fridge. Good vegetables to use are those which are firm, such as carrots, onions, mushrooms, celery, green beans, peppers, broccoli and cauliflower florets, leeks, radishes, spring onions, and bean sprouts. Mange-tout peas make a special treat and many interesting combinations can also include shredded green leaves such as cabbage and Chinese leaves. Experiment with whatever's in your store.

Serve the stir-fried vegetables with brown rice.

SERVES 4 AS AN ACCOMPANIMENT
OR 2 AS A MAIN COURSE

---

1 inch (2.5 cm) piece fresh root ginger
2–4 cloves garlic
1 green pepper, de-seeded and cut in strips
4 oz (100 g) green beans, cut in half or in strips
4 oz (100 g) broccoli florets
4 oz (100 g) mushrooms, quartered
2–4 oz (50–100 g) fresh or tinned whole baby sweetcorn (optional)
8 spring onions, cut in 1 inch (2.5 cm) lengths
3 tablespoons sunflower or nut oil
2 tablespoons soy sauce
1 tablespoon sesame seeds (optional)

Peel the root ginger and garlic and cut into thin slivers. Prepare the rest of the vegetables, keeping them whole where possible. Each vegetable or piece of vegetable should be about 2–2½ inches (5–6 cm) in length and not too bulky.

Heat the oil in a large frying-pan and begin by stir-frying those vegetables which require more cooking first, adding the others in the order of how long they will take to cook. Stir-fry until tender but still bright in colour and crisp. Add the soy sauce, sprinkle with sesame seeds (if using) and serve.

SPICED VEGETABLE POT

A mixed vegetable stew which can be made with the vegetables of your choice – whatever you have in stock. Select vegetables which you think will complement each other and avoid allowing one flavour to dominate. A stew such as this is an excellent way to use up left-overs. The hint of spice provides an exotic flavour and the cheese sauce turns it into a very substantial dish.

For convenience use a commercially prepared cheese sauce. These are available from supermarkets in cartons and tins and some are excellent. Use the equivalent number of cartons to give about 10 fl oz (300 ml) sauce and 2 oz (50 g) extra grated Cheddar cheese for the topping.

Serve with brown rice (see p. 93) and a cucumber and yoghurt salad.

SERVES 4

FOR THE VEGETABLES
2 tablespoons sunflower oil
1 large onion, finely chopped
2 cloves garlic, crushed
1 small red pepper
1 small green pepper
4 oz (100 g) mushrooms, sliced
1 courgette, sliced in rings
¼ cauliflower, broken into florets
½ teaspoon chilli powder
½ teaspoon ground cumin
2 teaspoons ground turmeric
Freshly ground black pepper
4 tomatoes, quartered

FOR THE CHEESE SAUCE
1 oz (25 g) sunflower margarine
1 oz (25 g) plain flour
10 fl oz (300 ml) milk, warmed
Pinch salt
Freshly ground black pepper
½ teaspoon English mustard
4 oz (100 g) Cheddar cheese, grated

Heat the oil in a large flameproof casserole and fry the onion and garlic until soft but not coloured. De-seed the peppers and cut into ½ inch (1 cm) pieces. If using a different selection of vegetables from those in the recipe, keep the size of each piece between ½ and ¾ inches (1 and 2 cm) when cutting up. Add all the prepared vegetables to the pan with the exception of the tomatoes and fry for a few minutes. Add the spices and seasoning and stir well to combine. Press a piece of greaseproof paper or foil on top of the vegetables and 'sweat' gently for about 20 minutes to draw out the juices, stirring from time to time. It is not necessary to add liquid: the vegetables will produce their own.

While the vegetables are cooking, prepare the cheese sauce. Melt the margarine in a saucepan, stir in the flour and mix to a thick paste. Remove from the heat and gradually blend in the warm milk, making sure that no lumps form. Return the saucepan to the heat and stir constantly until the sauce has thickened. Season with salt, pepper, mustard and half the grated cheese. Stir the tomatoes into the cooked vegetables. Pour the cheese sauce over the vegetable stew, sprinkle with the remaining cheese and brown under the grill. This dish can be made in advance and re-heated in the oven at gas mark 4, 350°F (180°C), for 20–30 minutes until bubbling hot and brown and crunchy on top.

SPANISH TORTILLA

The Spanish tortilla is a way of life in Spain and although simply a potato omelette it is loved and enjoyed by everyone. It is served throughout the day, cut in small pieces, as a snack, and as a main course in large wedges accompanied by fried sausages, bacon and peppers along with salad.

SERVES 4

4 tablespoons olive or sunflower oil
4 large potatoes, cut in ⅛ inch (3 mm) slices
1 large onion, thinly sliced
4–5 large eggs
Salt

Heat the oil in a very large frying-pan and add the potato slices one at a time. Alternate layers of potato with layers of onion slices. Cover the pan and cook the onion and potatoes over a low heat without colouring until the potatoes are tender, lifting and turning them occasionally. At this stage the potatoes will remain separate, not in a 'cake'.

Beat the eggs with a fork in a large bowl until they are slightly foamy. Season with salt to taste. Once the vegetables are soft and well cooked, drain them in a colander, reserving the oil for frying the tortilla. Then add the potatoes and onions to the beaten eggs, pressing them well down so that they are completely immersed. If possible, leave to soak for about 15 minutes.

Wipe the frying-pan clean and heat about 2 tablespoons of the reserved oil until very hot. Add the potato, onion and egg mixture, quickly spreading it out with a palette knife. Reduce the heat and cook very gently on a low temperature, shaking occasionally to prevent it from sticking. When the potatoes begin to brown underneath and shrink slightly from the edges of the pan, remove from the heat. Invert a plate slightly larger than the pan on top of the pan, tip the pan upside down and the omelette will fall on to the plate. Don't worry if the omelette sticks slightly to the pan when you turn it over – just scrape off the pieces and press them back into the omelette. Add another tablespoon of oil to the pan, allow it to heat thoroughly then, still working with speed, slide the omelette back into the pan to brown the other side. Alternatively, instead of turning the tortilla just slip the pan under a medium grill and cook until the surface of the tortilla is golden-brown.

When the omelette is cooked it should be golden-brown on the outside and moist and juicy inside. Transfer to a plate and serve hot or at room temperature, cut in wedges.

PIPERADE

This deliciously coloured Basque dish of peppers, eggs, tomatoes and garlic resembles scrambled egg but is much more exciting and substantial. It can be served hot with grilled bacon or ham, or cold cut into wedges with salad or stuffed inside a small length of garlic bread and taken on a picnic!

SERVES 4

4 firm ripe tomatoes
2 red peppers or 1 red and 1 green pepper
2 tablespoons sunflower oil
1 small onion, finely chopped
2 cloves garlic, crushed
1 teaspoon dried basil
8 large eggs
Pinch salt
Freshly ground black pepper
Triangles of toast, to garnish

Skin the tomatoes, cut in half, remove the seeds and chop the flesh roughly. Cut the peppers in half, discard the seeds and pith, and chop. Heat the oil in a large frying-pan and cook the onion and garlic until soft but not coloured. Add the tomatoes, peppers and basil and continue to cook for a few minutes until the vegetables are thick and pulpy.

Break the eggs into a bowl, beat with a fork and season with salt and pepper. Pour the eggs into the hot pan containing the vegetables and stir with a wooden spoon until the eggs start to thicken and become creamy. Take care not to overcook or the piperade will become dry and unappetising. Serve immediately on hot plates garnished with triangular pieces of toast arranged around the edge.

VEGETARIAN NIÇOISE SALAD

A vegetarian version of the famous salad from Provence which is generally made with tuna fish, anchovies and green beans. Mine is a slightly lighter version, but it can quickly be made more traditional (and substantial) with the addition of the tinned fish. Serve with French bread.

SERVES 4

A selection of mixed salad leaves, washed and dried
4 inch (10 cm) length cucumber, sliced in rings
2–4 eggs, hard-boiled and quartered
4 tomatoes, quartered
8 new potatoes, cooked and sliced
4 oz (100 g) Cheddar, Gruyère or Stilton cheese, cubed
16 black olives, stoned
2 tablespoons finely chopped fresh parsley
1 × 2 oz (50 g) packet garlic croûtons
French dressing, to serve

Arrange the mixed salad leaves on 4 large plates. Disperse the cucumber, eggs, tomatoes and potatoes among the leaves and scatter the cheese, olives, parsley and croûtons on top. Serve with French dressing (see p. 47).

PUDDINGS AND DESSERTS

There are many puddings and desserts that can be made from the store-cupboard; in fact the store-cupboard seems to lend itself to all manner of surprises, some more healthy than others. Many of my favourites use simple ingredients almost always available in the cupboard or fridge. Trifle sponges are a most valuable asset and along with a tin of custard, some tinned or frozen raspberries and a little sherry for added zest, they can be transformed into a delicious pudding in a flash. Tinned mandarin oranges and jelly make a quick children's favourite and the remains of the fruit bowl combine in individual ovenproof dishes with a layer of cream, a sprinkling of sugar and a few minutes under the grill to produce a memorable fruit brûlé. Then there are the light and luscious desserts quickly whipped into shape from a few fruit yoghurts or fools lurking in the refrigerator. The possibilities are endless and should certainly give vent to even the slightest creative urge.

The puddings and desserts I have included in this section are some of the ones I personally like best. Although not a fanatical pudding eater, I do enjoy the occasional Banoffi pie and iced lemon mousse at weekends and when entertaining. The rest of the week it's usually cheese and biscuits or fresh fruit. However, in the following pages there are many ideas for the sweet-toothed who get bored with just fruit.

SURPRISE ORANGES

An effective yet simple dessert of fresh and dried fruits, marinated in sherry and served in a hollowed-out orange shell – an exotic way to serve a fruit salad.

SERVES 4

4 large oranges
A mixture of fresh and dried fruits as available (such as green and black grapes,
apple, dates, berry fruits, banana and sultanas)
4 tablespoons sherry or fruit juice
Thin shortbread or wafer biscuits, to serve

Slice the flower end off each orange, leaving enough to form a container. Using a grapefruit knife, saw out the orange flesh: this will come out in one piece. Remove the membrane holding the segments together, along with any pith or pips. Cut the flesh into pieces and put in a bowl with the sherry or fruit juice.

Cut the fruit of your choice into pieces, discarding any pips and stones, and add to the bowl. Toss in the liquid, then pile into the orange shells. Set on individual plates and serve with thin shortbread or wafer biscuits.

MANDARIN DELIGHT

A perfect store-cupboard dessert and a children's favourite which can be made in minutes and needs only about 1 hour to set.

SERVES 4–6

1 × 11 oz (312 g) tin mandarin oranges
1 × 4¾ oz (135 g) packet lemon jelly
15 fl oz (450 ml) vanilla ice cream
Chocolate flake, to decorate (optional)

Drain the juice from the mandarin oranges and make up to 7 fl oz (200 ml) with hot water. Use this to dissolve the jelly. When the jelly mixture has cooled, whisk into the ice-cream until smooth. Add the mandarin oranges and pour into a 1½ pint (900 ml) glass bowl or spoon into individual serving dishes. Leave to set for about1 hour. Decorate with crumbled chocolate flake if using.

TRIFLING IN A TRIFLE

A quick store-cupboard trifle with an excellent flavour.

SERVES 4-6

1 packet trifle sponges (8 sponges)
1 × 11 oz (300 g) tin raspberries
3 fl oz (85 ml) sherry or fruit juice
1 × 15 oz (425 g) tin or carton ready-made custard
1 × 5 fl oz (150 ml) carton double cream (optional)
Glacé cherries and diamonds of angelica or grated chocolate, to decorate

Put half the trifle sponges in the bottom of a 1½ pint (900 ml) glass bowl. Pour the raspberries and their syrup on top along with the sherry or fruit juice, cover with the remaining sponge cakes and leave to soak for a few minutes.

Next, pour on the custard and leave to settle. Lightly whip the cream and spread half in a thin layer over the custard. Beat the rest until stiff and pipe rosettes around the edge. Decorate with cherries and angelica.

Alternatively, the trifle may be finished by spreading all the cream on top of the custard and sprinkling with grated chocolate. The cream can also be omitted completely and the surface of the custard sprinkled with chocolate only.

ETON MESS

A wickedly delicious way of using up broken meringues.

SERVES 4

1 × 5 fl oz (150 ml) carton double cream or fromage frais
1 × 11 oz (300 g) tin raspberries, drained
2 oz (50 g) broken meringues
Grated chocolate

Whip the cream until it holds its shape. Fold in the drained raspberries along with the meringue pieces. Pile into individual glass dishes and serve finished with a little grated chocolate.

RUM-BAKED BANANAS

When it comes to nutritional fast fruit desserts, bananas take the prize. They are the perfect packaged food.

SERVES 4
---

4 bananas
1 oz (25 g) dark soft brown sugar
Grated rind and juice 1 orange
¼ teaspoon ground cinnamon
4 tablespoons dark rum or sherry
Desiccated coconut, toasted, to garnish (optional)

Pre-heat the oven to gas mark 5, 375°F (190°C).

Peel the bananas and cut in half diagonally. Place in a shallow ovenproof dish. Mix the other ingredients together in a saucepan. Stir over a gentle heat until the sugar has dissolved, then pour over the bananas. Cover with foil and bake in the oven for 10–15 minutes. Serve sprinkled with coconut if using.

FRUIT AND NUT BANANAS

Serve these with fresh cream, yoghurt or vanilla ice cream.

SERVES 4
---

4 bananas
1 oz (25 g) dark soft brown sugar
Juice ½ lemon
4 oz (100 g) dried or fresh dates or mixed dried fruit
4 tablespoons dark rum
8 fl oz (250 ml) water
1 oz (25 g) ground almonds

Prepare the oven and bananas as described for rum-baked bananas (above). Heat the sugar, lemon juice, dates or mixed dried fruit, rum and water together in a saucepan and pour over the bananas. Sprinkle with the ground almonds, cover and bake in the oven for 15–20 minutes. Serve hot.

ICED LEMON MOUSSE

A delicious combination of mousse and ice cream, this tangy dessert can be made in advance and stored in the freezer until an instant pudding is required. It takes only 10 minutes to soften in the refrigerator before serving.

SERVES 4-6

Grated rind and juice 2 lemons
1 teaspoon gelatine powder
3 eggs, separated
4 oz (100 g) caster sugar
1 × 5 fl oz (150 ml) carton natural yoghurt
A few chopped nuts, to decorate

Begin by preparing the lemons. Use the fine part of the grater to grate the rind, making sure that the bitter white pith is not included. Then squeeze out the juice – you should have about 6 tablespoons.

Put 2 tablespoons lemon juice into a cup, sprinkle on the gelatine and leave for a few minutes until it becomes spongy. Place the cup in a small saucepan containing about 1 inch (2.5 cm) hot water. Stir over a low heat until the gelatine goes clear and liquid. Then remove from the heat and set aside to cool slightly.

Place the egg yolks in a mixing bowl and whisk, adding the sugar little by little, until the mixture is thick, creamy and increased in volume. Now gradually add the lemon juice, whisking constantly. Stir in the lemon rind and dissolved gelatine. The mixture at this stage should begin to show signs of setting. Stir in the yoghurt and 2 stiffly beaten egg whites. (The remaining egg white can be frozen and used along with others to make meringues.) Pour or spoon the mixture into 4 or 6 individual dishes or ramekins, put into the freezer and leave until frozen solid. When firm, overwrap and return to the freezer.

Ten minutes before serving, transfer the mousse to the refrigerator to defrost very slightly. Scatter the top with a few chopped nuts for decoration. Serve iced.

DRIED FRUIT COMPOTE

An excellent alternative to a fresh fruit salad, particularly in winter when the variety of fresh fruit available is less interesting. It is also a good example of a sweet dish where no sugar is added, the sugar occurring naturally in the fruit being enough. The compote can be served as either a dessert or breakfast dish. In fact it can be enjoyed as a nutritious snack at any time of the day and keeps for 3–4 days in the refrigerator – if it lasts that long!

SERVES 4

12 oz (350 g) mixed dried fruit (apricots, peaches, prunes, pears, dates, bananas or figs – which haven't been dipped in glucose and don't require soaking)
Grated rind and juice 1 lemon
15 fl oz (450 ml) unsweetened orange or apple juice
15 fl oz (450 ml) water
1 teaspoon ground cinnamon

Combine all the ingredients in a large saucepan, bring to the boil, then reduce the heat and simmer, covered, for 30–40 minutes or until the fruit is tender. Add a little extra juice or water if it begins to dry out. Serve hot or chilled.

FRUIT-FILLED MERINGUE

Commercially or indeed home-produced meringue shells are a great store-cupboard standby for the busy cook. They can be easily stored either in an air-tight container in the dry store-cupboard or in the deepfreeze. Defrost meringues at room temperature for 15–30 minutes before use. Ready-made chocolate cups can also be filled with the same mixture and are equally good.

SERVES 4

2 × 4½ fl oz (135 ml) carton fruit fool (such as apricot or peach)
A few chunky pieces fresh fruit (oranges are always a good standby)
4 meringue shells
Grated chocolate

Combine the fruit fools with the chunks of fresh fruit, reserving a few pieces of fruit for decoration. Pile inside the meringue shells and decorate with grated chocolate and the reserved fruit.

CHINESE GREEN FRUIT SALAD WITH GINGER

A refreshing and unusual sweet using whatever green fruits are available, either fresh or tinned or a mixture of both. A particularly successful combination is green gooseberries, pear quarters and lychees with a few fresh grapes for heightened colour. Jasmine tea is added to the sugar syrup along with thin slices of stem ginger to give an authentic Chinese flavour. For speed, cold jasmine tea can be used instead of the sugar syrup with a little ginger syrup from the preserved ginger jar added.

SERVES 4

FOR THE JASMINE SYRUP
4 oz (100 g) granulated sugar
10 fl oz (300 ml) water
Juice ½ lemon
5 fl oz (150 ml) cold jasmine tea
3 pieces ginger preserved in syrup, thinly sliced

FOR THE FRUIT
2 lb (1 kg) fresh green fruit (such as apples, pears, melon, grapes, kiwi fruit)
or tinned fruit of your choice

Put the sugar, water and lemon juice into a saucepan. Bring slowly to the boil, making sure that the sugar has dissolved before the water boils otherwise crystals will form. Boil for 1 minute. Add the strained cold tea and preserved ginger. Leave until completely cold. Prepare the fruit, cutting it into fairly large pieces, and drop immediately into the syrup to prevent discoloration. Chill thoroughly before serving.

CHOCOLATE MOUSSE

This is one of the richest and most delicious mousse recipes I know. A little goes a long way, so don't be tempted to serve larger quantities than I've allowed for in the recipe. Accompany the mousse with cigarette russe biscuits.

For a special occasion soak 4 almond macaroons in the rum, half-fill the mousse pots, set the soaked macaroons on top and cover with the remaining mousse – naughty but nice!

SERVES 4

4 oz (100 g) plain chocolate, broken into pieces
2 eggs, separated
1½ oz (40 g) unsalted butter, softened
1 tablespoon rum (optional)
2½ fl oz (65 ml) double cream, to decorate
Grated chocolate or chocolate curls, to decorate

Put the chocolate pieces into a bowl over a pan of hot water set on a gentle heat and stir until melted and smooth. (Alternatively, use a microwave oven, which is excellent for melting chocolate: allow 2½–3 minutes on full power, stirring every minute.) Remove the chocolate from the heat and beat in the egg yolks one at a time. The hot chocolate will help cook the yolks slightly. Beat in the softened butter and rum, if using.

In a separate clean dry bowl whisk the egg whites until they hold their shape, stir a little into the chocolate to thin it slightly, then fold in the remaining egg whites until evenly blended.

Pour the mousse into 4 small individual dishes or pots and chill until set. Beat the cream until it is stiff and pipe into rosettes on top of each mousse. Decorate with a chocolate curl or grated chocolate.

BANOFFI PIE

A truly shameful dessert but much loved even by the health-conscious.

Some recipes tell you to cook the unopened tin of condensed milk in a pan of boiling water for 2–3 hours until the contents are thick and fudgy in texture and colour. I prefer the taste produced by the more conventional method, which I give below, even though it requires additional sugar and butter and is a paler colour. It is useful, however, to have a few of the pre-boiled tins ready in the store-cupboard as the pie can then be made in minutes.

Warning: If you are going to boil tins of condensed milk, make sure that the water is constantly topped up and pierce holes in the tin. If the pan goes dry, the tin is likely to explode.

SERVES 4-6

FOR THE BISCUIT BASE
6 oz (150 g) digestive biscuits, crushed
3 oz (75 g) butter or block vegetable margarine, melted

FOR THE BANOFFI FILLING
1 × 14 oz (397 g) tin sweetened full-cream condensed milk
4 oz (100 g) butter
4 oz (100 g) caster sugar
1 ripe banana
Juice ½ lemon
1 × 5 fl oz (150 ml) carton whipping cream, lightly whipped (optional)
A little grated chocolate, to decorate

First prepare the biscuit base by mixing the crushed biscuits with the melted butter or margarine and pressing into the base and up the sides of an 8 inch (20 cm) loose-bottomed fluted flan tin to give a ¼–½ inch (5 mm–1 cm) thick 'lining'. Put in the refrigerator to set while you make the filling.

Combine the condensed milk, butter and caster sugar in a saucepan and stir over a low heat until the sugar dissolves. Bring to the boil and boil for 5 minutes only, stirring all the time. The colour will deepen slightly. Pour into the chilled biscuit base and, when cooled slightly, top with the sliced banana dipped in the lemon juice to prevent discoloration.

Just before serving transfer the pie from the flan tin to a plate. Cover the top with the cream, if using, and sprinkle with grated chocolate.

QUICK FRUIT BRÛLÉ

A quickly prepared and refreshing dessert of fresh, frozen or tinned fruit flavoured with liqueur or brandy, topped with thick cream, sprinkled with sugar and grilled until golden and crunchy on top.

A tin of dairy cream (with the liquid poured off) can be used instead of fresh cream, and if you're very health-conscious try fromage frais or set natural cow's or sheep's milk yoghurt instead of cream. A single type of fruit can also be used. Whatever combination you choose, you'll find they are all delicious.

SERVES 4

A selection of fresh or tinned fruit (such as peaches, nectarines, bananas, raspberries, strawberries, blackberries, blueberries, redcurrants, blackcurrants, oranges, pears, cherries or grapes)
Liqueur or brandy (optional)
5 fl oz (150 ml) double dairy or long-life cream
4 tablespoons demerara sugar

Pre-heat the grill until very hot.

Cut fruit such as pears, bananas, nectarines, etc., into slices or bite-size pieces, discarding cores and stones. If using tinned fruit, drain off the juice. Arrange the fruit in 4 individual shallow ovenproof dishes about 6 inches (15 cm) in diameter and 1 inch (2.5 cm) deep. Pour over a little liqueur or brandy, if using.

Whip the cream until it holds its shape. If using fromage frais or yoghurt, beat so that it will spread easily. Spoon over the fruit. Sprinkle with the sugar and brown quickly under the grill until golden and bubbly and only just warmed through. This takes only about 1 minute. Serve warm or chilled.

BLACKBERRY MOUSSE

A sharply flavoured fruit mousse prepared with fresh, frozen or tinned blackberries. The fruit is made into a rich purée with cream, lightened with egg white and gently set with gelatine. Any other berry fruits such as raspberries, loganberries or gooseberries can also be used.

SERVES 4

FOR THE FRUIT PURÉE
1 lb (450 g) fresh or frozen blackberries, defrosted if frozen
4 oz (100 g) caster sugar
Juice 1 small lemon

FOR THE MOUSSE
½ oz (15 g) gelatine powder
4 tablespoons water
1 × 5 fl oz (150 ml) carton double cream, lightly whipped
2 egg whites, lightly beaten

Put the ingredients for the fruit purée into a saucepan, reserving 4 whole berries for decoration. Simmer gently over a low heat for about 10 minutes to draw out the juices. Cool slightly, then press through a nylon sieve into a large bowl. This purée can be made in advance and frozen ready to be turned into a mousse in an emergency.

Soak the gelatine in a teacup in the 4 tablespoons water until spongy. Set the cup in a small saucepan holding about 1 inch (2.5 cm) hot water over a low heat. Stir until the gelatine is dissolved and clear. Slowly pour into the purée, whisking all the time. When the mixture begins to thicken and shows signs of setting, stir in the cream (reserving a little for decoration), then fold in the egg whites until both are evenly combined.

Pour into a serving dish and chill until set firm. Decorate with a few swirls of cream and the reserved whole blackberries.

GOOSEBERRY AND MANGO WHIP

The tartness of the gooseberries and the sweetness of the mangoes combine well to create this refreshing dessert which can literally be made in minutes. An even quicker alternative is to omit the tinned fruit and use two commercially prepared gooseberry fools mixed with chopped orange segments.

SERVES 4

1 × 11 oz (300 g) tin gooseberries in syrup
1 × 11 oz (300 g) tin sliced mangoes in syrup
1 small orange, peeled and cut into segments
1 × 8½ oz (240 g) carton Greek-style natural yoghurt
1 teaspoon caster sugar (optional)
Fine shreds orange rind, to decorate

Drain the syrup from the tins of fruit. Put the fruit into a liquidiser or food processor along with all but 4 orange segments, which should be reserved to decorate the dessert.

Process until the fruits are well blended but still have a slight texture. Fold in the yoghurt and sugar (if using) and divide between 4 individual serving dishes. Decorate with the reserved orange segments and a few very fine shreds of orange rind. Chill and serve.

INDEX